BY THE SAME AUTHOR

Hofmannsthal and Greek Myth (2002)
Sandy Denny: Reflections on Her Music (2011)
Becoming Helen Mirren (2019)
Laura Nyro: On Track (2022)

Frank Wedekind, *Franziska* (1998) [trans.]
Frank Wedekind, *Mine-Haha* (2010) [trans.]

Instead of a Critic: Essays Written and Unwritten

PHILIP WARD

The Minos Press

Published by The Minos Press, Cambridge,
England, 2022.

ISBN: 978-1-7396322-0-5

Front cover: Titania and Bottom, Take 1. Colour
chromo-engraving from the Complete Works of
Shakespeare published by John G. Murdoch, 1877.
Back cover: Titania and Bottom, Take 2. The
wedding of Jack and Marianne Mitford (*The Sketch*,
January 14, 1914).

Contents

Introduction

Years ago, in the pages of *The New Review*, I stumbled across the critic Ian Hamilton's obituary of his friend Francis Hope, who died aged thirty-four in a plane crash. I know very little about Hope, who hasn't even earned the posthumous glory of a Wikipedia entry, save that he published one book in his lifetime, a slim volume of verse called *Instead of a Poet* (1965). Hamilton's evocation of what might-have-been struck a chord. This modern-day Icarus sounded like so many of the Oxbridge literati I'd seen on the undergraduate launch-pad, maybe even a more versatile version of myself:

...If Francis had published his own book of essays, he might very easily have called it 'Instead of a Critic'. His short life often seemed like a junction of high roads not taken – or, more precisely, not altogether taken to. At Oxford in the late Fifties he had been everybody's tip for stardom: but as what? As a literary critic, a poet, a novelist, a politician, a historian, an all-purpose socio-cultural sage? No one knew where he was going: he was simply 'going far'. Later on, the same tipsters began wondering. All that brilliance, but no tomes. All that lightly-worn learning, but was not the lightness becoming more distinctive than the learning? All that irony and poise but nothing entirely non-ironical to show for it. 'Instead of' shades easily into 'if only'. If only he had laboured on that novel (those novels?), if only he hadn't been dazzled by Fleet Street and TV, if only he had been more (or less) – instead of more or less – left-wing. And sometimes it got personal: if only he were a touch more feelingful in manner, less nervous about seeming to have little nerve. Was it lack of courage, failure of ambition, or simply an undermining vein of lordliness?

We all have unlived lives. Mine are legion. And as writers we have unwritten books. The late George Steiner built an entire volume around this idea. "Each of these seven chapters tells of a book which I had hoped to write; but did not. It seeks to explain why" – so he tells us in the Introduction to *My Unwritten Books* (2009). Why were they unwritten? According to the blurb: "Because intimacies and indiscretions were too threatening. Because the topic brought too much pain. Because its emotional or intellectual challenge proved beyond his capacities." This is such a splendid notion it's tempting to imitate it. Lacking Steiner's planet-sized brain, I fear I am unable. Instead, I offer an attempt to pull together pieces I've written over the last twenty years or so in search of whatever links them, what Germans might call a *"roter Faden"*, a red thread. Some are achieved wholes, some mere abstracts for papers or tomes unwritten or unwritable. Some incline to the academic, others to the vernacular. When I submit academic articles, editors blue-pencil my "journalistic" turns of phrase. When I write for the market, my style is deemed "academic but accessible". Well, accessible is good: perhaps as good as it gets?

Instead of a Critic – I have the effrontery to bag the unused title – begins and ends with the 'two cultures' question, the relationship 'twixt arts and sciences. In between, the topics range from Anglo-German cultural relations and the refugee flight from Nazi Europe to myth and pictorial art. I touch on performance, whether in cinema, dance, 'straight' theatre or musical theatre. Along the way, an admiration for women as performers and writers diverts me somehow into modish considerations about gender fluidity. Certain authors' names keep popping up: Aldous Huxley, Rupert Brooke, Hugo von

Hofmannsthal, Frank Wedekind; a mixed bag, to be sure. Perhaps there is no red thread at all, only synapses, sites of transmission within my (sometimes) nervous system?

Aldous Huxley: Between Art and Science

In one of his early novels, *Point Counter Point* (published in 1928), Aldous Huxley introduces us to a gentleman-scientist called Lord Tantamount. In one scene we see Tantamount attending an orchestral concert. The aesthetic experience is first explained as "fiddlers [drawing] their rosined horse-hair across the stretched intestines of lambs". Then the narrator describes the physiological effect: the "shaking air rattled Lord Edward's membrana tympani; the interlocked malleus, incus and stirrup bones were set in motion... The hairy endings of the auditory nerve shuddered like weeds in a rough sea... and Lord Edward ecstatically whispered 'Bach!'" The abrupt move from physical event to his lordship's subjective reaction is meant to provoke surprise (and amusement?) in the reader; but it's also a bridge-building between disparate discourses. The making and reception of music can be reduced to a physical process, baldly described, without artifice – but to do so doesn't get us very far in describing how and why it moves the listener. Huxley was poised between art and science, determined to use one to illuminate the other.

It begins with his biography. Aldous Huxley was born in 1894 into a high-achieving dynasty. His grandfather was T.H. Huxley, the eminent Victorian biologist, educator and science writer, known as "Darwin's bulldog" on account of his proselytizing on behalf of Evolution theory. His great-uncle was Matthew Arnold, poet and influential cultural critic. (The relationship between those ancestors was important to him, as I discuss later.) So in his 'genes' he had a twin inheritance of sciences and arts. His brother was the biologist Julian Huxley, and Aldous himself had originally intended a medical career. This hope was dashed when he contracted an eye disease at the age of sixteen, *keratitis punctata*, which left him virtually blind for some months and, although he recovered partial sight, visually impaired for the rest of his life. He taught himself braille, read omnivorously, and started writing. Education was at Eton and Oxford. After a brief career as a schoolmaster back at Eton (where his pupils included Eric Blair, the future George Orwell) he carved out a career in the 1920s as a journalist and novelist. With those early novels – satirical, fizzing with ideas – he made a considerable impact. He married Maria Nys, a Belgian refugee whom he'd met during the First World War (his eyesight rendered him unfit for war service); they had one child, Matthew. After the early twenties they lived mostly outside Britain: France and Italy.

As the political climate darkened in the thirties, Huxley became more politically engaged, joined the Peace Pledge Union and espoused pacifism. This led him – in expectation of coming war – to emigrate to the USA in 1937, a decision that cost him some support at home. At the same time he was becoming ever more interested in religion and mysticism, what in one of his book titles he called the 'perennial philosophy'. (A key work here was his novel of the mid-Thirties, *Eyeless in Gaza*.) He settled in California. Like most European writers who landed in Los Angeles he was drawn to the film industry, wrote a number of film scripts but despite making friends among the Hollywood elite (Charlie Chaplin, Paulette Goddard, Greta Garbo, Anita Loos), he never fitted into the industry. One of his later novels, *After Many A Summer*, satirizes the emptiness of that Hollywood milieu. In the 1950s his continued interest in medical research brought a friendship with Dr Humphry Osmond, a psychiatrist specialising in schizophrenia. Under Osmond's direction Huxley began experimenting with hallucinogens. In the book he wrote about the experience, *The Doors of Perception*, he described how mescalin enabled him to discover what he called a "sacramental vision of reality", a biologically induced response that resembled the visionary insights he'd read about in religious texts. Later he extended these experiments to LSD. He was diagnosed with cancer in the early 1960s, and it was actually under the influence of LSD that he passed away in November 1963 – on the day of President Kennedy's assassination.

Thus he had the unusual distinction of becoming famous twice in his career. To a young generation in the 1920s he was the voice of cynical, disaffected post-war youth. In the late Fifties he embarked on a new career as public speaker, lecturing to large audiences on American campuses, on the subject of 'the human situation': religion, ecology, language, art, the unconscious. These lectures, and his writings on 'psychedelics' (a word that he and Osmond had coined), elevated him posthumously to 'guru' status for a new generation in the 1960s. And those who know their Beatles albums will recall he's one of the luminaries featured on the cover of *Sgt Pepper* (1967). It's even conceivable he might have a third 'coming' in our own time. When one reads his Cassandra-like warnings about the future of the planet, one sees prefigured many of the issues now central to the 'green' agenda.

This is from a letter of 1949:

If I had been able to go through with the biological and medical education, which was interrupted in my youth by a period of near blindness, this is what I should have liked to become – a fully qualified striker at the joints between the separate armour-plates of organized knowledge. But fate decreed otherwise, and I have had to be content to be an essayist, disguised from time to time as a novelist.

In the first of his *Human Situation* lectures he spoke of his own desire to be a "pontifex", a bridge-builder: "to build bridges between art and science, between objectively observed facts and immediate experience, between morals and scientific appraisals". He quotes a thought-provoking letter from his grandfather, T.H. Huxley, to Charles Kingsley (author of *The Water Babies*). T.H. Huxley wrote in 1860:

Science seems to me to teach in the highest and strongest manner the great truth, which is embodied in the Christian conception of entire surrender to the will of God. Sit down before fact like a little child, and be prepared to give up every preconceived notion, follow humbly wherever and to whatever abysses nature leads, or you shall learn nothing.

Aldous read this as a sign that the scientific process was "intrinsically an ethical process". Like anyone who'd lived through the Second World War (albeit, in his case, observed from the safety of the Californian hills), he was stunned by the potential of the atom bomb to bring about that 'apocalypse' he'd seen predicted in religious texts. A keen reader of scientific periodicals, he was very taken by a suggestion he found in the *Scientific Monthly* of September 1945 that all scientists should take the equivalent of a

'Hippocratic oath'. Just as physicians undertake to do no harm, so scientists should take a similar oath, such as:

I pledge myself that I will use my knowledge for the good of humanity and against the destructive forces of the world and the ruthless intent of men; and that I will work together with my fellow scientists of whatever nation, creed or colour for these our common ends.

This quotation occurs in a little tract Huxley published in 1947, *Science, Liberty and Peace*, one of many places where he grapples with this twin aspect of science, its capacity for good or ill. "As theory," he writes, "pure science is concerned with the reduction of diversity to identity. As a praxis, scientific research proceeds by simplification". This simplification is essential, he recognises, a necessary process of abstraction. Confronted by the data of experience, the scientist leaves out of account "all those aspects of the facts which do not lend themselves to measurement and to explanation in terms of antecedent causes rather than of purpose, intention and values." This makes perfect sense, he admits, because by this means we have achieved ever greater control over the energies of nature. But power isn't the same as insight. We run the risk of accepting "the world picture implicit in the theories of science as a complete and exhaustive account of reality".

Although his anxieties about science were sharpened by recent war and growing preoccupation with a 'numinous' reality that can't be tested in the laboratory, they run throughout his career and underlie his most famous book, *Brave New World* (1932). For what he shows there is what happens when the laudable processes of the experimenter in simplifying a problem in order to make it manageable are extended to society as a whole. The result is restraint, regimentation, curtailment of liberty and denial of individual rights. The book is still widely read, but it's worth reminding ourselves of some key elements. *Brave New World* is set in a World State centuries after some sort of cataclysmic war, where citizens are engineered through artificial fertilisation and childhood indoctrination into predetermined castes, Alpha, Beta etc, depending on their assigned future role in the society. "The principle of mass production at last applied to biology", as it's expressed in the opening chapter. The hero, Bernard Marx, is a misfit, an Alpha intellectual who, as a result of an accident during his bottling, lacks the physique of an Alpha and develops unorthodox opinions that set him apart from his fellows. The past has been abolished, in accordance with Henry Ford's dictum that "history is bunk". Likewise marriage: "Everyone belongs to everyone else". Promiscuity is the norm, enabled by universally enforced contraception. Most people remain in a state of infantile subservience, lulled into a state of bovine acquiescence by a diet of inane cinematic entertainment (the 'feelies') and endless sport (principally golf, a particular *bête noire* of Huxley's). The book is very funny and an opportunity for Huxley to ride many of his hobbyhorses, but it's also deadly serious in intent. Axiomatic in this future world is that "Happiness is the Sovereign Good". Medicine has advanced sufficiently to protect humankind from most illnesses; only death remains, converted into a kind of celebratory euthanasia. And when negative thoughts threaten, there is always a panacea, 'soma', the wonder-drug that restores happiness without side-effects.

Brave New World began life as a parody of H.G. Wells. Huxley was not convinced by the scientific optimism expressed in Wells's utopian fictions and determined to show what would happen when science ran amok. But as he confessed in a letter, he "got caught up in the excitement of his own ideas". He also got caught up in the events of the day. On a visit to England in early 1931 Huxley toured centres of heavy industry and even heavier unemployment, a tour that took him from the London docks and an East End abattoir to a Sheffield steelworks, a Durham coalmine and an ICI factory in Middlesbrough. Although he is often portrayed as a highbrow intellectual with a disdain for the 'masses', the articles Huxley wrote following these visits show him capable of empathy with people whose life circumstances were radically different from his own. This is important when one looks at the not-so-brave half of *Brave New World*. Not everyone lives under the new eugenic order. There are still 'reservations', fenced-off areas where humans live under the old dispensation – racked by disease, worshipping gods, entering exclusive marriages and giving birth naturally. Bernard, with his "pneumatic" girlfriend Lenina, visits a reservation in New Mexico and is there introduced to the novel's other main character, John the Savage, the accidental offspring of a Beta mother whose contraceptive measures failed. John, like Bernard, is an outcast who, when transported back to Bernard's world, looks with disapproval at everything he sees. He aches romantically for Lenina but when she offers him her body, he drives her away with cries of "whore" and "strumpet". For John, you see, has learnt his English from a volume of Shakespeare (conveniently discarded in the reservation) and through Shakespeare he has learnt to articulate all the emotions that have been banished from the brave new world: jealousy, mother-love, unsatisfied desire, divided loyalty. Mustapha Mond, World Controller, is one of the few Alphas permitted access to such obsolete literature and he explains to John why there is no place for Hamlet or Othello or King Lear in this brave new world:

"My dear young friend, civilisation has absolutely no need of nobility or heroism. These things are symptoms of political inefficiency. In a properly organised society like ours, nobody has any opportunities for being noble or heroic. Conditions have got to be thoroughly unstable before the occasion can arise..."

The Controller himself was a "pretty good physicist" in his time, we're told, but he has come to accept that research must be carefully limited: "We don't allow [science] to deal with any but the most immediate problems of the moment. All other enquiries are most sedulously discouraged". So it isn't only art that's incompatible with happiness, it's also science, unless it's carefully "chained and muzzled". In November 1935 a journalist asked Huxley whether in *Brave New World* "his ultimate sympathies were with the Savage's aspirations or with the ideal of conditioned stability" represented by the Controller. "With neither," he replied, "but I believe some mean between the two is both desirable and possible and must be our objective".

George Orwell sent Huxley a copy of *1984* on its publication in 1949. Replying, Huxley told him it was a "fine" and "profoundly important book" but disagreed with him on the outlook. "Whether in fact the policy of the boot-in-the-face can go on indefinitely seems doubtful." He believed the "ruling oligarchy" would always find "less arduous and wasteful ways of governing'; rulers will discover that the "lust for power can be just as completely satisfied by suggesting people into loving their servitude as by flogging and kicking them into obedience". In short, 1984 will always modulate into a Brave New World – the triumph of efficiency. Both novels have entered the public consciousness. Perhaps we see both forms of government in the world today?

When *Brave New World* was reissued in 1946, Huxley contributed a new Foreword, in which he said that if he were to rewrite the novel, he'd offer the Savage a third alternative: the option of living in a community where the economics would be at basis decentralist, the politics "Kropotkinesque" (i.e. anarchist) and where science and technology would be harnessed to serve rather than to coerce humankind. This notion stayed with him and he did eventually 'rewrite' the 'bad' utopia or 'dystopia' of the earlier book in the form of a 'good' utopia; this was his last novel, *Island* (1962). It's set on an imaginary island in the Indian Ocean called 'Pala' which has remained cut off from many colonial influences due to its lack of a decent natural harbour. A Westerner, Will Farnaby, is shipwrecked there after a visit to a neighbouring island which has not been so immune and has descended into military dictatorship. Pala is a symbol of the resolution of opposites, inhabited by an idealised Eurasian people who speak both Sanskrit and (conveniently) English and practice Mahayana Buddhism. Several generations earlier it had been visited by a Scottish doctor who settled there and formed a kind of alliance with the ruling Raja. In a symbolic meeting of East and West, old and new, this doctor, a scientific humanist, discovered the value of Buddhism while the Palanese Raja, the oriental mystic, discovered the value of pure and applied science. Together they forged a constitution for the island kingdom. "Wisdom," as Huxley puts it, "takes Science in its stride and goes a stage further." Much of the book consists of Farnaby, the Everyman figure, being taken on a tour of the island and initiated into its unique features by a series of lightly characterised locals. The plot, such as it is, culminates in the eventual takeover of this island paradise by the forces of the neighbouring island: there are natural resources to be exploited and Western interests to be appeased. But plot, never Huxley's strong point, is subordinate to the working out of concepts. As a novel, it fails on many counts. It perhaps works better as a kind of Platonic dialogue, standing or falling by the quality of its ideas.

The most striking aspect of *Island* is how the negative features of *Brave New World* have been refashioned to positive effect. Thus, instead of soma, the drug used for pacification and escape from reality in the earlier novel, the islanders use 'moksha', an enlightening drug taken cere-monially in rites of passage for mystical insight. (One of the most memorable things in *Island* is the long description of Farnaby's moksha trip, as he experiences loss of self and what Huxley calls "knowledgeless understanding".) Where the Brave New Worlders were forced to live communally to eliminate individuality, Palanese children grow up in 'Mutual Adoption Clubs', with parenting shared among the group. Birth control is freely available but not mandatory: the Palanese have never allowed themselves to produce more children than they could adequately feed, clothe, house and educate. At school, children are taught a form of birth-control at the same time as trigonometry and advanced biology. In their formal education the emphasis is placed firmly on the sciences of life and mind. Ecology is central to the curriculum, with examples like soil erosion and deforestation placed in the context of a universal morality: "Treat Nature well, and Nature will treat you well. Hurt or destroy Nature, and Nature will soon destroy you." The Palanese have adopted a selective attitude towards technology, concentrating on means to improve agriculture, medicine and nutrition. They have no need for the large-scale research required to support heavy industries mass-producing consumer goods and armaments. A Palanese elder explains:

Lenin used to say that electricity plus socialism equals communism. Our equations are rather different. Electricity minus heavy industry plus birth control equals democracy and plenty. Electricity plus heavy industry minus birth control equals misery, totalitarianism and war.

It's not clear what role the arts play in this island paradise. They have landscape painting, which encourages the viewer to "perform an act of self-knowing". By their isolation the Palanese people have avoided the two characteristically European ideologies of Christianity and Freudianism. Greek tragedy reaches the island only to be laughed at. In one bizarre scene Will Farnaby attends a marionette show, 'Oedipus in Pala', which ends with a boy and girl managing to talk Jocasta out of suicide and Oedipus out of hanging himself by telling them "not to be silly". Elsewhere, Peter Pan is judged to be suffering from an "endocrine disbalance". In his memoirs, quoted at various points in the novel, the Old Raja, who co-founded the present order, cannot see how to reconcile a doctrine of the oneness of all things with what he knows of the conflicts underlying Western art: "Dualism... Without it there can hardly be good literature. With it, there most certainly can be no good life."

On Pala the mynah birds have been taught to intone the word "Attention!" It's the first word that Farnaby hears when he regains consciousness on the beach after his shipwreck. The intention is that we attend to all those things the brain customarily screens out. One of the educators Farnaby meets on the island explains that "by themselves the humanities don't humanize. They're simply another form of specialization on the symbolic level". Huxley became obsessed by the need for what he called "non-verbal humanities, the arts of being directly aware of the given facts of our existence". He mapped out plans for educational reforms involving specific training of the "mind-body", most importantly in the field of perception. "Seeing is, like talking and walking, a learned activity," he said. Much of this comes from this own visual impairment and the remedies he sought to overcome it. He even wrote a book, *The Art of Seeing*, about the techniques he'd tried to dispense with spectacles. (Early photos of Huxley show him wearing thick pebble specs; in later pictures he's without glasses.)

It's only in this last novel that Huxley introduces sympathetic scientist-figures – medics versed in holistic therapy, technologists dedicated to the public good. Earlier novels portray scientists as childlike, or cold and lacking in emotional intelligence. In *Antic Hay* (1923) we meet Shearwater, who becomes an image of futility when he ends up cycling on a stationary bike in an experiment to measure sweat; he becomes, in other words, "sheer water". Another novel, *The Genius and the Goddess* (1955), purports to be the biography of a physicist, Henry Maartens, described as "an idiot where human relations were concerned, a prize ass in all the practical affairs of life". Like Shearwater he is cuckolded by a more desirable male. A decidedly sinister figure is Dr Obispo in *After Many A Summer* (1939), who is employed by an ageing Californian millionaire to find medical means to stave off death; Obispo won't let morality – or anything else – get in his way.

Near the end of Huxley's life he got caught up in a contemporary debate about the so-called 'Two Cultures'.

This originated in a public lecture given in Cambridge in 1959 by C.P. Snow – a public figure, administrator and novelist who enjoyed some reputation at the time. Snow's thesis was that, as intellectual disciplines, science and the humanities had become split into 'two cultures', each neither trusting nor understanding the other. He condemned the British education system as having, since the Victorian era, over-rewarded the humanities (especially Latin and Greek) at the expense of scientific and engineering education. This, in practice, had deprived British elites (in politics, administration, and industry) of adequate preparation to manage the modern scientific world. He called for an end to specialisation in schooling at age 16 as a first step towards orientating Britain towards a shiny, technology-led future.

Snow's diatribe prompted a furious response from the famous and tetchy Cambridge don, F.R. Leavis, for whom to study Literature was to study Life itself. Leavis lashed out at the "intellectual nullity" of Snow's "panoptic pseudo-cogencies", arguing (if that's the word for such *ad hominem* invective) that, whatever Snow's claim to authority as a scientist, "as a novelist he doesn't exist; he doesn't begin to exist". Huxley's response, however, was to stand above the fray, rejecting both what he called the "bland scientism of [Snow's] Two Cultures" and the "ill-mannered, one-track, moralistic literarism" of Leavis. In his own book, his last, *Literature and Science* (1963), he preferred to look back nearly a century to a debate between two of his eminent ancestors. T.H. Huxley, in a lecture of 1880, issued a challenge to the defenders of traditional classical education. Science, he insisted, formed part of culture and made an indispensable contribution to the national good. This jibe was aimed at, and two years later responded to by, Matthew Arnold. A training in the natural sciences, said Arnold, might produce a practically valuable specialist, but it could not turn out an "educated" man. The battle lines were drawn long before Snow or Leavis. Huxley traces the divide further back still – to Charles Darwin, who recounts in his autobiography how, as a young man, he'd taken pleasure in the poetry of Milton and Wordsworth, but in his later twenties lost the "aesthetic taste" and felt only intense boredom when he tried to reread Shakespeare. Or, on the other side, to William Blake who could never forgive the scientists for analysing the divine mysteries into "the Atoms of Democritus and Newton's Particles of Light". Or Keats, who complained of explanations that would "conquer all mysteries by rule and line" and "unweave a rainbow". But Huxley found an early ally in Wordsworth who, while accepting an emergent two-cultures division, looked forward to their fruitful co-operation.[1]

Thus Huxley's 1963 book, *Literature and Science,* is his final attempt at *rapprochement* between these two 'cultures', which corresponded to two sides of his personality and two sides of his family inheritance. He reasons that the goal of science is to describe the physical universe in irreducibly public terms, while the very different but complementary goal of literature is to explore and describe the irreducibly private world of psychological and spiritual experience. The book discusses the different ways in which scientists and poets use language, concluding that "Man cannot live by contemplative receptivity and artistic creation alone... he needs science and technology." He concentrates principally on the failure of writers to reflect the extraordinary scientific developments of the modern world rather than rebuking

---

[1] For a fuller discussion of the 'Two Cultures' controversy and its nineteenth-century antecedents, see the final essay in this book.

scientists for neglecting the insights of art. A contrast is drawn between Dante, whose cosmology in *The Divine Comedy* although obsolete is highly precise, and the Modernist poets of the 1920s, from whose writings "you would be hard put to it to infer the simple historical fact that they are the contemporaries of Einstein and Heisenberg". He has a long quote from Werner Heisenberg. It reads in part:

Modern science shows us that we can no longer regard the building blocks of matter, which were considered originally to be the ultimate objective reality, as being things 'in themselves'… that is to say independent of our observation. Rather we now find ourselves in the midst of a dialogue between nature and man, a dialogue of which science is only one part…

Heisenberg goes on to talk about of the inappropriateness of conventional notions of objective and subjective, outer and inner, which has a familiar ring to Huxley. It reminds him of utterances of poets and mystics. He looks forward to the arrival of "some great artist" who'd achieve the task of incorporating "the hypotheses of science into harmonious, moving and persuasive works of art".

I feel there's something 'utopian' about this programme of synthesis. He repeatedly castigates modern writers for their ignorance of science. It should theoretically be possible to make poetry out of anything, he says, noting elsewhere that "Chaucer is as much at home among the stars as he is among the birds and beasts and flowers of earth". But with Chaucer, as with Dante, his example is drawn from the Middle Ages. How far, in the modern era of specialisation, anyone (even a planet-sized brain like Aldous Huxley) could command vastly diverse areas of knowledge is a moot point.

A recurrent idea in his essays is to view human beings as what he called "multiple amphibians": living a "strange existence… inhabiting, without being completely at home in, half a dozen almost incommensurable worlds – the world of concepts and the world of data, the objective world and the subjective, the small bright world of personal consciousness and the vast, mysterious world of the unconscious." We seem to have an intellectual instinct to "impose order upon confusion, to bring harmony out of dissonance, and unity out of multiplicity". A "Will to Order". In the realms of science, art and philosophy its workings are "mainly beneficent". But in the social sphere, the realm of politics and economics, that Will to Order becomes dangerous, reducing human diversity to sub-human uniformity and freedom to servitude. "The beauty of tidiness is used as a justification for despotism."

We can't articulate any of this but through the imperfect medium of language. As a writer, he was aware how words are never enough. One of his characters comments that: "Love is always accompanied by events in the nerve endings, the skin, the mucous membranes, the glandular and erectile tissues. Those who don't say so are liars. Those who do are labelled as pornographers." We need another set of words, he suggests, "to express the natural together-ness of things". He playfully suggests new words like "muco-spiritual" or "viscerosophy". One aim of education should be to bring realisation of "the part played by language as a virtual philosophy, a source of ontological postulates, a conditioner of thought and even perception, a moulder of sentiments, a creator of behaviour patterns."

In making sense of our multiple lives, we need the 'two cultures' in complementarity: "Literature, art, music are not sophistry and illusion, but simply those elements of experience which scientists chose to leave out of account, for the good reason that they had no intellectual methods for dealing with them." Arts, philosophy, religion, he suggests, are efforts to "describe and explain the non-measurable, purely qualitative aspects of reality". The scientist has no right to claim that his product of specialisation is a complete picture of reality. Arts and sciences are means to an end, not ends in themselves.

Huxley approaches the "multiple amphibian" in multiple ways. As well as considering what humans are and can yet be, he looks back to what they have been. Charles Darwin famously suggested that "our ancestor was a hairy quadruped furnished with a tail and pointed ears, probably arboreal in his habits". In his exchange with Huxley's grandfather, Matthew Arnold quoted this line, observing that "this good fellow" the hairy quadruped, nonetheless "carried hidden in his nature... something destined to develop into a necessity for humane letters". Aldous Huxley's characters are often caught between their caveman ancestry and their civilised present. Such ambivalence of perspective has caused readers to see him as a misanthropist. Sometimes they have a point. The final, grotesque scene of *After Many A Summer* is pessimistic indeed. Dr Obispo travels to England where he discovers the Fifth Earl of Gonister, now 201 years old and living locked in a dungeon with a female housekeeper whom he brutalises. The Earl had discovered centuries earlier an 'elixir' for prolonging human life; unfortunately, it also sends evolution into reverse and the gibbering Earl is now reduced to a "foetal ape".

Evolution can be the stuff of science fiction, even if here he posits the absurdity that a million years of evolution can be reversed in the space of a hundred years. However, evolution as fact cannot be denied. Huxley drew very close to D.H. Lawrence in the final years of Lawrence's life. It's a fascinating friendship. An 'odd couple', if ever there was one: the highly cerebral scion of the upper middle class and the passionately driven miner's son from Nottinghamshire. And they clashed over science. "All scientists are liars," Lawrence would declare when Huxley brought up some experimentally established fact not to the other man's liking. They once had a long argument about evolution, a theory in which Lawrence fervently disbelieved. "But look at all the evidence," Huxley insisted. Lawrence's answer was characteristic: "But I don't care about evidence. Evidence doesn't mean anything to me. I don't feel it *here*." And he pressed his two hands on his solar plexus. Huxley abandoned the argument. Lawrence, he recognised, was quite intelligent enough to grasp scientific method, but it was "incompatible with the exercise of his gift". Where the scientist's aim was to "push back the frontier of the unknown", Lawrence's aim was "to remain as intimately as possible in contact with the surrounding darkness". Taken altogether, what Huxley's writings suggest is that, by judicious combination of arts and sciences, we may be able to know both the darkness and the light.

(With thanks to Dr Grahame Danby and the Crystal Scientifique group.)

***

In August 1916, Huxley, newly graduated from Oxford, enjoyed a boozy lunch in London with his cousin by marriage, the lawyer E.S.P. Haynes. After polishing off the Chablis and "talking of liberty and sex and the decadence of the Huns in loud resonant voices", they repaired to Lincoln's Inn

where out of strong boxes, come all Rupert Brooke's papers with dozens of unpublished poems, which a less intoxicated man would have read with ease, but which to me seemed somehow rather hieroglyphic, though ultimately their meaning was never hidden to me... but it was trivial stuff, some of it rather funny, though, and all testifying to the various amours of the beautiful Brooke in all the continents of this and several of the other planets. (A.H., letter to Frances Petersen, 23.8.1916)

***

Rupert Brooke

In 2015, among so many solemn centenaries of the First World War, we remembered the ill-fated Gallipoli landings – part of a campaign, intended to knock the Ottoman Turks out of the war, which cost the lives of so many British and Empire servicemen. The soldier-poet Rupert Brooke never made it to the landings. Bound for the Dardanelles, his troop ship was moored off the Greek island of Skyros when he developed septicaemia from an insect bite and died. He is buried on the island. In following years, Brooke, "the handsomest young man in England" in the opinion of W.B. Yeats, has become a poster-boy for the Lost Generation.

Although still best remembered as a poet, Brooke was also a sharp-eyed critic and travel writer, with interests in literature, theatre, art and politics. Over a century after his death, interest in his life and work continues unabated. Yet, for all the attention given to his poetry and colourful private life, another aspect of his work has been neglected: his activity as essayist, polemicist and critic. Brooke was not only a poet but also an aspiring academic and a founder member of the Marlowe Dramatic Society at Cambridge, with interests both in the rediscovery of Elizabethan and Jacobean drama and in contemporary European theatre. He was alert to new currents in painting, particularly Expressionism and Post-Impressionism and a regular reviewer of new poetry (where his tastes were more conservative). As a Fabian socialist, he was keen to propagandize for the cause. As a traveller, he reported with wide-eyed enthusiasm on his impressions of North America and the South Seas. Taken together, these writings form a microcosm of British intellectual concerns in the years before the First World War and present an alternative to the jingoistic image of the soldier-poet that took root so soon after Brooke's premature death at the age of twenty-seven.

**

His connections to Cambridgeshire (my home county) are well-known. In 1909 he took lodgings in Grantchester in a former farmhouse called The Orchard (doubling as a tearoom even then) before moving next door to The Old Vicarage a couple of years later. Early in 1912, frustrated in love and thwarted in his bid for a Fellowship at King's College, he suffered some form of nervous breakdown. Recuperation abroad was recommended, and in May we find him in the Café des Westens in Berlin, seated at a table by the window, reminiscing about his skinny dips in Byron's Pool:

Here I am, sweating, sick, and hot,
And there the shadowed waters fresh
Lean up to embrace the naked flesh.

'The Old Vicarage, Grantchester', from which these lines come, has become one of his most famous poems, a deft combination of nostalgia, luxuriant language and whimsy that stays just this side of sentimentality. Or so I would argue. George Orwell was less impressed:

Rupert Brooke's 'Grantchester', the star poem of 1913, is nothing but an enormous gush of 'country' sentiment, a sort of accumulated vomit from a stomach stuffed with place-names. Considered as a poem 'Grantchester' is something worse than worthless but as an illustration of what the thinking middle-class young of that period felt it is a valuable document. ('Inside the Whale' [1940])

My impression is that Orwell was a sensitive reader of other writers. As a thinker of the Left, he was naturally suspicious of writers who didn't share his politics, but he was also a big enough critic to appreciate literary quality wherever it surfaced. If he didn't find literary quality, he still recognised that a writer could be read historically as a voice of his time – which seems to be his approach to Brooke. The long, nuanced essay he wrote on Kipling shows all these strategies in play. Conversely, a writer could be on the same side of the political fence as Orwell but still be chastised for irresponsibility. A few pages after his comment on Brooke in 'Inside the Whale', he takes a pop at Auden. In Auden's poem 'Spain' there's a reference to "necessary murder". Orwell doubts that Auden had seen murder at first hand: "Mr Auden's brand of amoralism is only possible if you are the kind of person who is always somewhere else when the trigger is pulled". Yet, overall, Orwell declares the poem to be "one of the few decent things that have been written about the Spanish war". But I digress. Back to Brooke's poem and his "accumulated vomit from a stomach stuffed with place-names". As a Cambridgeshire resident of twenty years standing, I'm perhaps more attentive to these place names than Orwell was (he was living in Hertfordshire in early 1940 when his essay appeared).

Brooke's strategy is first to contrast England, where an "unofficial rose" blooms under an "unregulated sun", where feet may trespass on the grass, with the Teutonic passion for order and regulation:

… and there are
Meads towards Haslingfield and Coton
Where *das Betreten*'s not *verboten*.

Then he narrows his focus to tell us why, of all Cambridgeshire villages, he prefers "the lovely hamlet Grantchester". By contrast, he says,

… Barton men make Cockney rhymes,
And Coton's full of nameless crimes,
And things are done you'd not believe
At Madingley on Christmas Eve.

In the margin of the manuscript Brooke wrote a list of villages to be worked into the poem. Comberton was on the list but didn't make the final cut, being replaced by Trumpington. Denis Cheason, in his book *The Cambridgeshire of Rupert Brooke*, suggests that Brooke may not even have visited all the places he mentions. In any case, we locals are not to take offence:

To those of you who are residents of the villages, do not be dismayed by Rupert Brooke's comments. He was only joking, or perhaps belittling neighbouring villages to highlight the Grantchester which he loved.

No offence is taken, for the choice of names is very obviously driven by the rhyme scheme: "Coton/*verboten*", "rhymes/crimes". But could there be any more behind it? In her slim volume on the history of The Old Vicarage, Mary Archer concedes that the place names "appear to have been chosen more for convenient scansion than for any accurate local allusion". However, she goes on to suggest possible, if far-fetched, sources for the references to Barton and Madingley. For Barton she quotes the anonymous ballad 'The Knocking Ghosts of Barton', which is almost in the same octosyllabic metre as Brooke's poem:

Jiminy, criminy, what a lark,
You must not stir out after dark,
For if you do you'll get a mark –
From this knocking ghost of Barton.

And of Madingley it is said that, in the late nineteenth century, a Rector of High Church leanings promised the villagers a High Mass on Christmas Eve. The squire forbade his tenants to attend but they went, defiantly, and were turned out of their homes on Christmas Day. It's the sort of story that might have appealed to Brooke, had it come to his ears. But neither Mary Archer nor Francis Burkitt and Christine Jennings, in their book *Rupert Brooke's Grant-chester*, have any suggestions for Coton. Another work, *Coton Through the Ages* (Kathleen Fowle and others, 2013), lists a number of crimes and misdemeanours over the centuries – at least one case of arson and a fair bit of sheep-rustling – but I don't see anything likely to tickle the fancy of the "handsomest young man in England".

So do these place names go down in the annals of literature merely as handy rhymes? As "accumulated vomit"? Or are we missing a trick here?

***

In December 1909 Rupert Brooke reviewed Ezra Pound's new collection, *Personae*. It was a meeting (in print) between two poets of very different hue:

Mr. Ezra Pound's work was 'discovered' recently by certain London papers, and, a little timorously, acclaimed as valuable and inspiring. He is – do not his name and his verse betray it? – a young American; and he writes *vers libre*. His virtues and faults are both obvious. He is blatant, full of foolish archaisms, obscure through awkward language not subtle thought, and formless; he tastes experience keenly, has an individual outlook, flashes into brilliance, occasionally, and expresses roughly a good deal of joy in life. The dedication of the book is very pleasant, and oddly expressive of the author's character. "This book is for Mary Moore of Trenton, if she wants it." The abandon, the suggestion of jolly power, and the slight posing of that, are typical of his character. When Mr. Pound writes notes, and in some of his poems, the posing, the unnecessary assumption of a twisted Browningesque personality, it is exceedingly tiresome. But when inspiration cleans him a little of that, and when he writes in metre, the result is quite good. He writes a 'Ballad of the Gibbet', in which his 'persona' is the sixth of the companions of Villon on a famous occasion. [...]

There, in spite of the affectation of 'disdeign', one cannot but feel a note of exultation that is rare enough in modern poetry, whether written by the young or by the middle-aged. But though in this, and in other metrical poems, Mr. Pound shows he is a poet, he has fallen, it appears, under the dangerous influence of Whitman, and writes many poems in unmetrical sprawling lengths that, in his hands, have nothing to commend them. In these forms he generally, not always, fails to express much beauty. He rather wantonly adopts them, no doubt, in youthful protest against the flood of metrical minor verse of today. A little quiet reasoning is all he needs. For the truth of the matter is very clear. There are certain extremely valuable 'aesthetic' feelings to be got through literature. These can be got, it is empirically certain, sometimes through prose, of the ordinary and of the Whitmanic kind, often and more intensely through poetry, in which the three elements of thought, words, and metre are employed. That is the beginning and end of the whole affair. The only especial note to be made in the case of Mr. Pound is that he sometimes uses a poetical variety of prose which is metrical in so far as it is composed entirely of iambic feet, but not in so far as it pays no attention to lines. The lengths are chopped off anyhow. It is certain now (thanks in part to Mr. Saintsbury), as it has long been obvious, that the foot is immensely important in English prosody. It is still more certain that the line is. Otherwise *Lorna Doone* and much of Dickens would be pure verse.

Mr. Pound has great talents. When he has passed through stammering to speech, and when he has more clearly recognised the nature of poetry, he may be a great poet. It is important to remember his name; and we shall be made to recognise it when he turns from prose, admirable prose as it sometimes is, to confine himself to the forms in which he wrote 'Camaraderie'. [...]
(*The Cambridge Review*, December 2, 1909.)

The American poet Ezra Pound (1885-1972) arrived in London in August 1908 and made the city his home for much of the next twelve years. There, as Brooke comments, his early work was often well received.[2] *Personae*, Pound's third volume of poetry, appeared in April 1909. The Latin title referred to the donning of masks by players in the classical theatre and Pound used the poems to try out a variety of voices and techniques learnt from earlier poets reaching back to the Provençal troubadours. He also drew on Robert Browning's employment of the dramatic mono-logue. Brooke, an early – though questioning – admirer of Browning, was clearly unimpressed by Pound's adoption of a "twisted Browningesque personality". Moreover, Brooke was no friend of free verse and detected the "dangerous influence" of Walt Whitman in Pound's "unmetrical sprawling lengths". His emphasis here on the foot as the unit of poetic metre would be amplified in a later review of George Saintsbury's *History of English Prosody* (1911).

In a postcard postmarked 19 October 1909, written while he was at work on the Pound review, Brooke refers jocularly to Pound as "the most modern of modern poets" and then (mis)quotes a line from 'Revolt Against the

---

[2] See *Ezra Pound: The Contemporary Reviews*, ed. Erkkila.

Crepuscular Spirit in Modern Poetry', another poem from *Personae*. (Pound's line "Great God, if these thy sons are grown such thin ephemera..." becomes Brooke's "Almighty God, that thy spawn should be such ephemera!")

Brooke and Pound first met in London on 16 December 1909 shortly after this review had appeared. Since it was signed 'R.B.' it is unclear whether Pound knew that Brooke was the author. Despite the reservations expressed in Brooke's review, the two poets continued in a state of mutual guarded admiration. When Edward Marsh was compiling the first *Georgian Poetry* anthology in autumn 1912, Brooke persuaded him to invite Pound to contribute. (Pound was unable to oblige, for copyright reasons.) Pound, meanwhile, was hedging his bets and meeting with Hilda Doolittle ('H.D.') and Richard Aldington in the British Museum tearoom to launch a rival movement, to be known as 'Imagism'.

A minor spat broke out in late 1912 in the pages of *Poetry Review* when Pound wrote dismissively of several of Brooke's fellow British poets, prompting Brooke to a defensive response. Yet, after Brooke's death in 1915, Pound praised him as the "best of the younger English, though [T.S.] Eliot is certainly more interesting." He was "infinitely better than his friends", Pound opined, although it was a matter of regret that he "flocked with the stupidest set of Blockheads to be found in any country", the likes of Lascelles Abercrombie and John Drinkwater.[3] In the face of Brooke's posthumous canonisation, Pound wrote to Harriet Monroe, "it might seem time for him to be protected by people like myself who knew him only slightly".[4]

---

[3] Letter quoted in Stock, *Life of Ezra Pound*.
[4] Pound, *Selected Letters*, 12 October 1915.

Bloomsbury

Rupert Brooke had once been close to the Bloomsbury set. The War changed all that, or at least confirmed the deepening rift. While he found (most of) them pleasant and remarkable as individuals, the staunch patriot in him lamented the "subtle degradation of the collective atmosphere" they embodied. Estrangement was especially distressing to Virginia Woolf, who liked him very much.

The best thing I've read on 'Bloomsbury' is the little volume with that title by Quentin Bell, who was both Virginia Woolf's nephew and her first biographer. He represents this privileged faction – the Woolfs, the Bells, the Stracheys, the Keyneses – as engaged in a short-lived social and intellectual experiment. In their effort to "live a life of rational and pacific freedom, to sacrifice the heroic virtues in order to avoid the heroic vices, Bloomsbury was attempting something which, to the next generation, seemed unthinkable." During the First World War, "it was still possible for an intelligent man or woman to be neutral". With the advent of Fascism, he argues, Bloomsbury was confronted with a quarrel in which "neutrality was impossible". The surviving Bloomsberries had no answers.

Life in Squares, the BBC's racy dramatisation of the Bloomsbury set which aired in 2015, struggled to put such subtleties on screen, preferring to confine itself to the sexual shenanigans among these free spirits. It did, however, remind me of one of my own early attempts to break into the literary world. This would be about 1983. Christopher

Howse, a college contemporary, even then sporting a Shavian beard, half-hunter watch in his waistcoat, had landed a job at the *Catholic Herald* – Books Editor, I think, or Literary Editor – and offered me reviewing work on the paper. I was not and am not of the Pope's party, but my agnosticism seemed to be no barrier. As far as I remember, only two books ever came my way. One was *Andrina*, a volume of short stories by the Orcadian writer George Mackay Brown. The other was a volume of Virginia Woolf's Letters, newly available in paperback. The first review was published only after the newspaper's editor stumbled across it when he was clearing out Christopher's desk following the latter's career-enhancing departure to the *Daily Telegraph*. The second appeared more promptly. It doesn't seem *bad*...

The Flight of the Mind: The Letters of Virginia Woolf. Volume I: 1888-1912, (Chatto & Windus)

"Do you think all the lower classes are naturally idiotic?" writes the 26-year-old Virginia Stephen to Saxon Sydney-Turner, betraying the prejudices of her age and class. The appearance in paperback of the Virginia Woolf Letters is a major publishing event, but I suspect that this first volume of Nigel Nicolson's edition will provide more nourishment for the biographer than the *littérateur*. Indeed, it takes us only as far as the publication of her first novel, *The Voyage Out*. Virginia was a tireless correspondent, above all to her sister Vanessa, and the 638 letters printed here, while they show the informal shaping of that familiar prose style, so hectic yet thoughtful, make better evidence for the breathless vitality of a young woman coming of age – not yet a novelist. "Nessa and I have been arguing the ethics of suicide all the morning, as we are alone, and what is an immoral act," she writes prophetically in April 1905. But these young ladies were not often alone. Their lives were fashionably filled with dinner parties and romancing; by letter 600 Virginia is equivocating over Leonard's marriage proposal, asking only "that you should leave me free, and that I should be honest." The complete Letters, with their authoritative editor's introductions and excellent footnoting of personalities and events, are more than the sum of their parts, but this first part makes an adequate *hors d'oeuvre*.

Rosamond Lehmann

Does the impulse to create alternative worlds take characteristically different forms in fiction by men and women? We might provisionally call these 'utopian' and 'allotopian' (from Greek *allos* + *topos*, other place.)[5] A very rough distinction, if it be admitted at all, as there are, undoubtedly, 'utopian' fictions by women (e.g. Charlotte Perkins Gilman) and, perhaps, 'allotopian' fictions by men.

Utopian fiction by men (from Thomas More to H.G. Wells) typically presents an 'engineered' world, an elaborated construct of town planning, legal systems, technological innovation, eugenics. In women's writing a more subjective tradition prevails, born of frustration with the obligation upon women until very recent times that they adapt themselves to their environment without expecting to influence it or shape it. This 'allotopian' tradition was always dismissed by male historians and critics. Thus Frank Manuel, noted historian of utopianism, reading the Duchess

---

[5] Umberto Eco introduced the term 'allotopia' into literary discourse in an essay 'I mondi della fantascienza' (in *Sugli specchi e altri saggi. Il segno, la representazione, l'illusione, l'immagine*, 1985): "Allotopia presumes that our world is really different from the actual one and allows the occurrence of things that do not usually happen (i.e. animals speak, magicians or fairies exist), that is, it constructs an alternative world and implies that it is even more real than the real one, to the point of convincing the reader that the fantastic world is the only one true. A typical allotopia allows the once imagined storyworld to dissolve any connections with the reality, with the obvious exception of allegorical narratives."

of Newcastle's *Description of a New World* (1666), found in it a utopia "so exclusively personal" as to border on the "schizophrenic", a "solipsistic manifestation" which could never be a "shared dream" and thus join the "mainstream of utopian feeling".

I detect the 'allotopian' impulse in Rosamond Lehmann's work – thinking especially of her first and last books. In *Dusty Answer* (1927), Judith Earle, "hot for certainties", believes finally that she has rid herself of the "futile obsession of dependence on other people. She had nobody now except herself, and that was best." Not a "solipsistic" conclusion, but probably a misplaced hope, for, in Lehmann's novels, her heroines' striving for autonomy is always thwarted by the enfeebling effect of external realities. By the end of her life Lehmann had discovered "worlds within worlds", astral planes of alternate reality, inaccessible to ordinary senses, where the dead, her young daughter among them, come to life (*The Swan in the Evening*, 1967). Conscious that "human kind / Cannot bear very much reality", she is consoled by a visionary world. From the vigorous responses of her (predominantly female) readership one might conclude that she was tapping a "mainstream of utopian feeling", not by the proposed re-engineering of given reality but by depicting, through fiction, a "voyage in" to self-knowledge and by intuiting, through autobiography, an alternate reality between the interstices of everyday life.

(Note: Please regard the foregoing as an exercise in *faux* scholarship.)

Katherine Mansfield and Germany

Katherine Mansfield's first published book of stories, *In A German Pension* (1911), was inspired by her stay in the Bavarian spa town of Bad Wörishofen in 1909. The 21-year-old was taken there by her mother after falling pregnant by a lover. That is how these things were managed in those days (didn't our own dear Julian Fellowes crib this plotline for an errant daughter in *Downton Abbey*?) Smuggle the girl away from moral disapproval to a foreign land where no one knew her and she knew no one. In the event, Mansfield sadly lost the baby. Nonetheless, she used the opportunity of an enforced eight-month stay to observe German manners, pretensions and sensibilities from close-up. True, Germany never held the same spiritual hold on her as France, the country where her life came to a premature end in 1923, but German culture and the German language continued to fascinate her.

Although she never carried a baby to full term (and may have been rendered infertile by her many health problems), Mansfield has not lacked for literary progeny, in Germany as elsewhere. In her journals around 1920 she noted that nowadays selves are two a penny, we seem to have hundreds of selves: "what with complexes and suppressions, and reactions and vibrations and reflections – there are moments when I feel I am nothing but the small clerk of some hotel without a proprietor who has all his work cut out to enter the names and hand the keys to the wilful guests". Interiority is called into question: do we possess such a thing as one true, continuous identity? This fracturing of selfhood may help to explain why, as a posthumous presence, she is able to creep so easily into other people's fictions and autobiographies.

The process of reincarnation began with D.H. Lawrence's *Women in Love* (1920), in which Gudrun, one of the two Brangwen sisters, is given many characteristics of the Mansfield Lawrence knew (as well as a German forename). A recent example is Kirsty Gunn's *My Katherine Mansfield Project* (2015), a singular amalgam of memory and fiction, research and journal. Mansfield's spectral afterlife reached a sort of peak in the 1980s when, in the German-speaking world, no fewer than three novels appeared representing divergent responses to the New Zealander. In Erwin Einzinger's *Kopfschmuck für Mansfield* [Head-dress for Mansfield] (1985) – perhaps the most manipulative of the three – a (male) narrator becomes obsessed with Mansfield and co-opts her writing difficulties and practices as a spur to his own blocked creativity. *Die Kränkung* (1987; translated as *Quotations of a Body*, 1998) by fellow Austrian Evelyn Schlag is the story of a decaying relationship in which the first-person narrator interprets her life with the aid of an imagined character called 'Kathleen'. Details from Mansfield's biography and writings are woven into the text. So strong is the narrator's identification that 'Kathleen' is at once companion, literary mentor and *alter ego*. Christa Moog's *Aus tausend grünen Spiegeln* [From a thousand green mirrors] (1988) edges closer to autobiography as Moog writes about her life in the former East Germany, her move to the West and subsequent visits to sites associated with Mansfield. In all three novels identification with Mansfield is expressed through quotation, allusion and parallelism. However, where Schlag fictionalises a real person, Moog extends self-representation by imaging her own biography alongside that of a great predecessor. All three novels pose the same question: Where are the boundaries between fiction, biography and autobiography?

Kafka: The Significance of Clothes

In March 1908 Franz Kafka made his first appearance in print with a series of prose sketches under the collective title *Meditation*. On first publication the individual pieces were untitled, but republishing some of them two years later in the Prague newspaper *Bohemia*, he added titles and chose to call one of them 'Clothes'. Since this piece was extracted from an earlier effort, 'Description of a Struggle', composed in 1903-4, it must count as the earliest appearance of a subject which was to recur in his work right down to the final pages of *The Castle* (1922). Given that Kafka's father, Hermann, kept a shop in Prague specialising in fashion accessories, the subject must have had strong biographical roots.

'Clothes' is not a story so much as a philosophical reflection. It invites the reader to perform a thought-experiment which is then written up in the form of a literary experiment. Clothes adorning beautiful bodies become creased and dusty; therefore no one would dream of wearing the same dress every day. And yet pretty girls appear every day in the same body, their "natural fancy dress"; only by evening do their faces look used, no longer wearable. It is an experiment in chiasmus, rhetorical reversal. Instead of presenting us with people and then demonstrating how their appearance is mediated through dress, Kafka takes us in the opposite direction. He begins with clothes, apparently disembodied, then imagines them fitted over anonymous bodies. Only later is a wearer mentioned, who, characteristically, is "niemand" ("nobody"), that absent personality who in another striking piece from the same collection, 'The Excursion into the Mountains', is willed into existence by the constant reiteration (and occasional capitalisation) of the word "Niemand". When the girls finally make their appearance in 'Clothes', it is in a new paragraph beginning "And yet", thereby placing them in stark antithesis to their clothes, which have been made antecedent to them.

Thus in a very early piece we see two characteristics of Kafka's art already working together: the assimilation and adaptation of rhetorical forms and the rawness of the unexpected, or unexpectedly intense, perception. To most of his readers it would never occur to separate clothes from wearers in a way that makes the relationship between them reversible, but to Kafka such thoughts were native. In a diary entry of 10 April 1922 he recalls being told as a boy that the women who appeared to him the best-dressed were supposed to be bad – an interesting observation from the period when he was at work on *The Castle*, in which the protagonist K is perpetually suspicious of women like the landlady of the Herrenhof Inn whose clothes seem too good for their station in life. An earlier diary entry, of 31 December 1911, recounts how the son was always badly dressed as a schoolboy, in clothes run up by his parents' customers:

I naturally noticed – it was obvious – that I was unusually badly dressed, and even had an eye for others who were well dressed, but for years on end my mind did not succeed in recognising in my clothes the cause of my miserable appearance. Since even at that time, more in tendency than in fact, I was on the way to underestimating myself, I was convinced that it only on me that clothes assumed this appearance, first looking as stiff as a board, then hanging in wrinkles.

The clothes only looked bad because *Kafka* was wearing them: it is the same association – and dissociation – of ideas as in the later entry. To be well-dressed is not necessarily to be virtuous; to be without virtue – a nothing, a "Nichts" – is necessarily to be badly-dressed. There is ample biographical evidence that Kafka felt alienated from his body to an unusual degree. He would write of it as if it were something apart from himself: "It is certain that a major obstacle to my progress is my physical condition. Nothing can be accomplished with such a body. I shall have to get used to its perpetual baulking" (*Diary*, 21 November 1911). These feelings are shared by Eduard Raban, the protagonist of one of Kafka's earliest fictions, 'Wedding Preparations in the Country'. Raban is travelling, with extreme reluctance, to a meeting with his fiancée. Oppressed by the rainy weather and the apparent demands made on him by undemanding passers-by, he takes refuge in a childhood fantasy: "I don't even need to go to the county myself, it isn't necessary. I'll send my clothed body." While his besuited double stumbles down the stairs, Raban himself will remain tucked up in bed transformed into a beetle – a creature, we may reflect, not burdened by self-consciousness or the necessity to get dressed in the morning. And just as a character's body may be something apart from him, so his clothes may appear poorly appropriated to his body, like the hard, round hat of the Inspector in *The Trial* which its owner places carefully on his head using both hands "as one does when trying on new hats", or Frieda's cream-coloured blouse in *The Castle* "which sat strangely on her poor body".

Clothes without bodies are often a cause of anxiety in the fiction. When in *The Trial* Josef K faints after his first visit to the court offices, it is attributed in part to the stifling effect of washing hung out to dry. When Karl Rossmann enters Brunelda's room in *Amerika* he at once notices how dark and stuffy it is, a result of, among other things, the hanging clothes. Fräulein Bürstner in *The Trial* also leaves clothes lying around – or one item, at least, a white blouse – which troubles Josef K, her fellow lodger, when he is seeking to reconstruct the circumstances of his arrest for his own benefit and re-enact them for hers later that day. He first notices the garment hanging on the window catch when he is ushered into the Inspector's presence. After the officials have departed, Fräulein Bürstner's room, which they had requisitioned on K's account, is restored to its previous state. Frau Grubach, his landlady, is satisfied that everything is in order and the tenant herself assures him that she has noticed nothing out of place. Yet the over-zealous restoration had tidied the blouse from its place at the window, a tiny detail which Josef K nonetheless thinks important enough to mention.

A special case that repays examination is that of clothes which are themselves bodies, parts of animal bodies: furs. In *The Metamorphosis*, Gregor Samsa's most cherished possession is a photograph that he has cut from a magazine and framed, depicting a lady in furs. He is so proud of this photograph that, when later in the story his mother and sister invade his bedroom to clear out the furniture, hoping thereby to facilitate his new hobby of climbing on the walls and ceiling, he covers it with his body to prevent its removal. He suspects a plot by his sister to prise him from the wall: "He'd sooner spring into Grete's face". Only the sight of his mother collapsed in shock at an accidental glimpse of him awakens sentiments of filial love stronger than his attachment to the picture ("there'd still be time to save the picture") and he crawls after his sister, thinking to give her advice as in the old days. The most obvious interpretation of Gregor's behaviour is that, having been excluded from the "human circle" by his transformation from man to insect, he clings, literally as well as metaphorically, to any vestige of his human past. But might the *subject* of the picture also be significant? Much has been made of Kafka's interest in Sacher-Masoch's *Venus in Furs*, that bestseller of *fin-de-siècle* eroticism, implying that by depicting a classic object of fetishism (fur) the photo itself becomes a fetish object. But, more than a source of pleasure, fur was a locus of anxiety for this author. Some clue may be found in a letter Kafka wrote in May 1914 to Grete Bloch. In it he explained that, even though she was the confidante of his soon-to-be fiancée Felice Bauer, he was suspicious of her at first on account of her furs: "I believe it's called a stole or similar, this item of clothing". At issue was not whether the garment suited her, but that Kafka did not *like* it. It reminded him of nomadic hunters. He disliked the artificiality of the flattened pelt with its silk lining; he would have preferred fur on both sides, which he recognised was an impossibility. He could not separate the image of the fur from the image of her person and suffered particular torment when she played with the ends of the garment. He could only breathe again when he finally saw her in a fine travelling coat, at last without furs, "truly freer, purer, brighter": "But it was already too late. Today you might have been wrapped in 500 such pelts and I'd dare to free you from them all". Several ideas are in play here. There is the abhorrence (more familiar in our time than in Kafka's) of the sensitive vegetarian for the wearing of animal skins. There is a notion that the animal character of the original has been traduced by its silk lining, while in its place is found an artificial "flexibility and adaptability", a sorry

43

counterfeit of its original protective function as the human wearer holds an end to her mouth to ward off the fog. Returning to *The Metamorphosis*, we find a similar figure in Gregor's photograph: the heavily fur-clad lady who holds out her muff towards the spectator. In a story about a man who is involuntarily reduced to animal status, Kafka selects this image of Man's wilful dominance of the animal world. There is a parallel example at the very end. The Samsas' charwoman arrives, bursting to tell the family how Gregor's body has been disposed of. The narrator comments how "the almost upright small ostrich feather in her hat, which had irritated Mr. Samsa during her entire service with them, swayed lightly in all directions." Doubtless, Gregor's father is irked by the affectation of the feather, but at the same time we are reminded how elements of the animal world are constantly recruited into our own by dress.

Where there are clothes without bodies we may also expect to find bodies without clothes. In the *Letter to His Father* Kafka recalls the horror of sharing a bathing-hut with his powerfully built father and the relief he felt when the latter undressed first, leaving his son alone and able to postpone indefinitely "the shame of a public appearance". The association of nakedness with humiliation and degradation is an obvious cultural one. The condemned man in 'In the Penal Colony' is "naturally naked", the Officer tells the Traveller long before the nature of the punishment and therefore the necessity of nakedness is explained. The miscreant court officials subjected to flogging in *The Trial* must strip themselves entirely, while the Flogger himself is dressed in some form of dark leather gear which leaves his body half exposed – a suggestion here of the mildly pornographic which recalls Josef K's earlier discovery that the law books to which the Court presumably turns for precedents are, in fact, collections of erotica depicting, typically, a man and woman sitting naked on a sofa. To be undressed or semi-undressed is to make oneself a laughing-stock, like Robinson in *Amerika* who stands in his underwear in the street trying vainly to cover himself with a sheet from the Hotel Occidental but still exposing himself to ridicule. Above all, it is to be *powerless*. In *The Castle* K falls asleep in Bürgel's bedroom and dreams he is fighting with a naked Castle secretary. In losing his clothes, the secretary loses more, his dignity and his ascendancy over K, and thus in dream K can achieve what is never possible in waking – a fight with the Castle on equal terms. That clothes confer power is a fact well-known to Josef K also. On his first encounter with the merchant Block, a fellow accused, he is surprised that anyone should think to pursue a legal claim in his shirt-sleeves, a fact which he emphasises by catching hold of Block by the braces as he stands before the Judge's portrait: "Merely by being in possession of a thick overcoat he felt his advantage over this thin little man." (Presumably this is the same comforting outerwear on which the humiliated warder Franz had dried his tears before the flogging.)

So much for the multiple relationships between clothes and their wearers in Kafka's work. Enumerating them demonstrates the 'significance' of clothes in one sense, their importance as measured by the number and variety of references to be found. But in what other sense are they 'significant'? Are clothes carriers of *meaning* for Kafka, and if so what meaning(s) do they carry? In the tradition of Realistic fiction from which he inherited, clothes were frequently indicators of social position. As a social being, albeit a highly unusual one, Kafka himself relied on conventional assumptions about dress. At his first meeting with Felice Bauer, recorded in his diary on 20 August 1912, he mistook her for a maid: "She looked very domestic in her dress although, as it later turned out, she by no means was." In other words, he assumed that she *was* what she looked like: indeed, he reached an "unshakeable verdict" on her. In the more speculative environment of the fiction these assumptions survive but become harder to read. When the family in *The Metamorphosis* loses its breadwinner, the mother is forced to go out to work and she finds it sewing underwear for a dress shop. The choice of detail to indicate downward social mobility would not look out of place in nineteenth-century fiction: it rhymes pleasingly with her son's reminiscence of wooing a cashier from a hat shop. The story assumes the existence of a hinterland service economy beyond the Samsa flat, and both characters are drawn to its clothing sector.

More problematic, however, are the litigants crowded into the court precincts in *The Trial*:

All of them were carelessly dressed although the expressions on their faces, their bearing, the style of their beards and many small details which were hard to identify showed that they belonged to the upper classes.

This passage presupposes a whole anthropology of dress and appearance which is not supplied from within the novel, a fact confirmed by the generic reference to "small details" which it is not necessary to itemise, but at the same time undermined by the phrase "hard to identify"("*kaum sicherzustellend*"). It is as if Kafka wants to affirm the existence of a typology of appearance but leave the individual values open: to work, as it were, in algebra rather than arithmetic. We sense this more clearly in *The Castle*, a novel which is felt by many to create a more self-sufficient world of meanings than the earlier works. On the very first page, K is awoken by a young man in "city clothes". Since the village setting has been established in the opening sentences, this detail marks him as a representative from Outside, even if Kafka then characteristically calls his credentials into question by giving him an "actor's face". Later in the novel there is a refinement of the town/country distinction when a stream of customers is admitted into the taproom wearing "provincial rather than peasant dress", implying that there are social gradations within rural society as much as in urban. Kafka dies not specify what peasant costume looks like but we may assume that it is loose-fitting since representatives of the Castle (like the court officials in *The Trial*) wear fitted clothes, as Olga explains to K: "The most striking thing about their clothes is that they're mostly close-fitting, a peasant or artisan wouldn't have any use for such garb." It is by this means that Kafka signals to the reader, long before it is apparent to K, that the assistants assigned to him are not 'his' at all but emissaries of the Castle.

Elsewhere there is a distinct emphasis on appropriateness of dress. In *The Trial* the court official's wife is being courted by the examining magistrate, whose love tokens take the form of stockings which, she regrets, are "too fine and not suitable" for her. Pepi in *The Castle* wears a totally unsuitable dress after her promotion to barmaid which she has tried to tighten, presumably in pursuit of a more womanly profile, but with results that are "childishly inept... her clothes were laughable, she had evidently dressed according to her inflated ideas of the significance of a barmaid." In general, then, clothes are expected to be appropriate to the wearer rather than to the purpose. Indeed, we find examples of clothes which serve no purpose. The "black, close-fitting" attire of the arresting officer in *The Trial* is one such: it is equipped with pleats, pockets, buckles and buttons, "all of which gave the impression of being very practical but without making it very clear what they were actually for." Another such item is Robinson's waistcoat in *Amerika*: it has false pockets, the prime feature of a garment of which he is so proud that he keeps puffing up his chest in order to draw attention to it. Again, a diary entry may come to our aid here. On 2 January 1912 Kafka recalls another of the manifold humiliations of his adolescence: his resistance to being fitted for a dress suit, in which he would be able to cut a dash at dances. After an argument with the tailor, they settle on a tuxedo instead, but young Kafka specifies a design which the tailor has never heard of and cannot imagine any application for ("it couldn't be worn for dancing," he complains). There follows an abortive trip to a shop where Kafka remembers having seen such a garment displayed – it has since disappeared from the window – the pair return empty-handed and Frau Kafka tells her son that by his action he will be forever banished from "girls, an elegant appearance and dances." Thus clothes become the outward manifestation of inner reality, or, in the words of Kafka scholar Wilhelm Emrich, "symbols of the individual's mental and spiritual condition". The appropriate clothes for someone who is empty, void (*"nichtig"*) would be clothes that do not exist, just as the appropriate coat for a minor functionary in an inscrutable judicial machine would appear "practical" but betray no hint of what purpose it might serve.

There are also clothes which are appropriate to the time of day. In *The Metamorphosis* Gregor's father was accustomed, before his son's transformation, to slouch around the flat all day in a dressing gown, to lie "buried in bed" long after his son had left the house. When Gregor is transformed, so are family relations and so is his father. The balance of power is reversed; now Gregor is confined – buried in effect – in his bedroom, while his father struts around in his bank uniform. For Kafka, the bed is a place charged with possibility – a place for getting better, a place for getting worse, somewhere to have sex, somewhere to die – so we should not be surprised to find a proliferation of references to night attire. In *The Trial* Josef K is arrested in his nightshirt and puts his trousers on as a first step to, as he imagines, taking control of the situation. The painter Titorelli, on the other hand, a Court employee, remains in his nightshirt all day, although he tries in vain to button it up when receiving visitors. Clearly, Kafka is here investing him with 'bohemian' characteristics and implying that he enjoys closer relations with the female "brats" who cluster around the door to his studio than he admits to, but it is another reversal of expectation for Josef K, typical of the chiastic judicial process in which he is bound up. In the same novel we notice how Fräulein Bürstner returning late at night from the theatre receives Josef K in her bedroom, standing by the bedpost but not removing so much as her hat. This is in pointed contrast to his regular partner, the night-worker Elsa, who receives his visits during the day while still in bed, someone therefore whom he has probably never seen in a hat.

Uniforms present a special case in appropriateness. The Officer in *In the Penal Colony* admits that his full-dress uniform is much too heavy for the tropics but he wears it as a reminder of home. When Gregor Samsa attempts to leave his room to explain himself to his boss, his eyes alight on a photograph of himself from military service days, demanding that respect be paid to his lieutenant's uniform.

With the symmetry already noted in *The Metamorphosis*, this detail is echoed later when his father acquires "a tight blue uniform with gold buttons". Unlike Gregor's, however, this is not a uniform to compel respect (although it clearly helps his father to regain his *self*-respect). So proud is he of it that he will not take it off even at home – inappropriateness again – but sits around "as if he were always ready to do his duty". As a result the uniform, which was not new to begin with, becomes worn and dirty, in fact reminiscent of the unsavoury bell-hop's uniform that Karl has to wear in *Amerika*, which particularly under the shoulders is now "damp beyond drying from the sweat of the lift-boys who had worn it before him." If clothes are the outward sign of the inner person, then uniforms are potentially the opposite. They are form preceding content. Karl's uniform, in the words of Kafka scholar Ritchie Robertson, shows how he has been "squeezed into a ready-made slot in society with only the most perfunctory attempt to adapt it for his individual needs". Josef K in *The Trial*, whose thoughts run in rigid categories, ready-made slots, cannot accept his arresting officers as genuine because they are not in uniform, but as the Inspector explains: "We could be wearing uniforms as proper and exact as you like and your situation wouldn't be any the worse for it." He later discovers that the officials signal their identity in subtler ways, by wearing badges of varying size and colour on their collars or, in the Court servant's case, by customising his civilian clothes with the addition of gilt buttons lifted from an officer's coat. Indeed, it is difficult to obtain official dress from the administration. That is why the lower officials organised a collection among themselves to buy a set of smart clothes for the Clerk of Inquiries, the one official who is in constant contact with all parties to legal proceedings.

A much more detailed account of a prevailing dress code is provided by Olga in *The Castle*. From her we learn that her brother Barnabas's striking white winter coat which K had at first mistaken for official dress is, in fact, something made for him by their sister Amalia. Barnabas has been promised an official suit but it has not arrived – a fact which calls into doubt his status as "messenger". On the other hand, there is no Castle livery: the officials and higher servants wear their own clothes; certainly, the inferior servants wear "official suits" but these take many forms. If Barnabas received his official suit, it would not only confirm him in office, it would also define which part of the officialdom he belonged to. Olga discounts the possibility that her brother might be one of those higher servants who do not wear official suits anyway. Again, we encounter this idea that clothes are somehow an emanation from within, so that, despite all variations of dress, "one always recognises a servant of the Castle straightaway by their clothes."

So far we have accumulated examples and discussed particular forms of dress and we have speculated on clothes as bearers of particular meanings. It is time to step back and consider a broader significance for clothes in the writer's *oeuvre*. Edwin Muir said of Kafka: "He sees everything solidly and ambiguously at the same time; and the more visually exact he succeeds in making things, the more questionable they become." This is a constant feature of his writing from the beginning, but beside it we might note an evolution which begins in 'Naturalism', passes through 'symbolism' and ends in something like 'allegory'. These terms are best kept in inverted commas because they have been much argued over by Kafka scholars. In the early writings one is struck by, on the one hand, the profusion of closely observed detail – a legacy, it has been suggested, of exposure to Flaubert's travel journals – and, on the other, an intensity of perception unique to Kafka. The early, unfinished story 'Wedding Preparations in the Country' (1907-8) is a good example. Eduard Raban steps out of his front door and at once his senses are assaulted from every direction. In an orgy of perception he notices everything, even if everything is nothing more than passers-by engaged in the act of passing by, the details of which Kafka catalogues with a sort of mesmerising pedantry. Here is a great deal about clothes – at least twenty references in the whole story – but are they significant? The vast majority probably not; they are the detritus of Naturalism, description pursued for its own sake in a rambling narrative which seems as unconcerned to reach a destination as its hero. But one detail stands out. Early on, Raban is troubled by a bystander who has lifted her gaze from her shoes and brought it to rest on himself, or possibly the rain, or possibly a small sign under which he happens to be standing. In his subsequent daydream, a fantasy of omnipotence, he determines to put a stop to such random invasions of privacy: "Drivers and walkers are shy, and every step they want to take forward, they request of me by looking at me." The look of indifference which the woman turned on him will be replaced by a look of supplication. Now her previous action in looking at her shoes seems more carefully selected: it is a gesture of modesty which Raban would endorse, and since it is her shoes that will do the walking when Raban gives permission, it is a very apt place for her to look. The excitement of perception is well illustrated by another of the pieces in the *Meditation* volume, 'On the Tram', which Kafka placed either before or after 'Clothes' in different editions of that collection. It describes a girl glimpsed on a streetcar.

Her clothes are minutely observed, but since the description is introduced by the remark "she is as distinct to me as if I had run my hands over her", it might be said to be viscerally 'motivated' in a way that the twenty-odd hats, coats and skirts of 'Wedding Preparations' are not. There exists a ludicrous allegorical interpretation of this piece by someone [Kurt Weinberg] who assumes that the girl who stands on a tram must stand *for* something and accordingly equates her left hand with Judaism, her five fingers with the Pentateuch. But Kafka supplies a conclusion in his last paragraph: how can she *not* be as amazed at herself as the narrator is, as he has demonstrated himself by his evocation of her transitory presence.

Critics seem to agree that Kafka completed his literary apprenticeship with the writing of 'The Judgment' in 1912. He intimated as much himself in an oft-quoted diary passage of 23 September 1912 after finishing the story: "Only in this way can writing be done... only with such a complete opening of the body and soul." Certainly, the stories and novels after that date show a higher level of integration. We can see this in his treatment of clothes in the 1914 story 'In the Penal Colony'. Here is no rag-bag of hats and coats but a skilful deployment of clothes as and when the plot requires it. At the very beginning of the story we are given an incongruous detail: the Officer has stuffed two ladies' handkerchiefs behind his uniform collar. We hear no more of them until the Officer undresses prior to his own execution, whereupon they fall from his collar and he returns them to the prisoner, from whom they had been confiscated as "presents from the ladies". Now, these are not, like the dropped handkerchief in *Othello*, an engine of the plot, but they are in no sense extraneous to it. The return of these items forms part of the transfer of power from

Officer to prisoner and of the sudden reversal in the latter's fortunes, but in addition they are invested with symbolic importance: in Edwin Muir's terms they are at once "solid" and "ambiguous". As favours from the Commandant's ladies they can be freighted with whatever significance the ladies possess in the story; and they can plausibly bear this weight because they are metonymic images – part of the ladies' accessories. They embody the "new lenient administration", just as their owners do. Other items of clothing assume similar importance in the story. Before being placed in the machine, the prisoner is forcibly cut out of his clothes by the soldier, in obvious contrast to the Officer who, when his turn comes, undresses himself, handling each item very carefully after removal. In both cases the discarded clothes end up in the ditch. When he is reprieved the prisoner reassumes his clothes, garments which were never meant to be worn again. They look comic, being "cut in two up the back". The shirt had been used to wipe his vomit from the machine; now it must be washed in the basin which the Officer had repeatedly used for absolution but now no longer can. These plot details involving clothes exactly mimic the transactions between characters in the story and the shifting balance of power. Something similar happens in *The Trial* where the arresting officers begin by confiscating Josef K's clothes pending the outcome of his trial, whereas their counterparts in the last chapter fold his clothes carefully, "as if they would still be needed, albeit not in the near future." Sometimes a garment has a symbolic significance which is private to the owner. Such is Gardena's wrap in *The Castle*. It is a present from the high official Klamm – beautiful, she thinks, although to K it is nothing but an unremarkable woollen shawl – and possessed of healing powers. When she puts it on "all suffering seems to be taken away from her".

Kafka's last novel, *The Castle*, has often been held in the past to be an allegory. If clothes receive allegorical treatment, this is where we should expect to find it. Klamm, the elusive figure whom K spends much of his time trying to contact, is described as being infinitely variable in all reported aspects of his appearance: "only in respect of his dress are the reports consistent, he always wears the same clothes, a long black tail-coat." All these varied accounts are attributable, we are told, to the varied moods and expectations of those who never catch more than fleeting sight of the man. Klamm, it seems, has accomplished what was only a hypothesis in the early piece 'Clothes': he manages to change all aspects of his appearance from day to day *except* his clothes. These clothes represent his unitary function; they are the visible sign of his transcendent authority. In contrast to those pathetic individuals – Karl Rossmann, Samsa senior – who forced their bodies into second-hand uniforms, Klamm's black attire is the one immutable outward manifestation of what he *is*. What it is that he is is, thankfully, beyond the scope of this essay to answer, but to call his function allegorical seems too reductive.

Kafka's manuscript of *The Castle* ends, before the short incident with Gerstäcker, with a lengthy discussion between K and the landlady of the Herrenhof on the subject of... clothes. It is prompted by K's observation that the landlady is inappropriately dressed for her job and for the time of day (two points noted above): she appears in an "evening dress" in early morning. The landlady thinks he is laying claim to a false knowledge of clothes. He denies it. Each accuses the other of untruthfulness about his or her occupation. K suggests that she is aiming at something else, to which she replies with strange intensity: "My only aim is to dress nicely, and you are either a fool or a child or a very evil, dangerous person." The obvious gloss on this passage is that K has now been accepted into the village on his own terms, so much so that the landlady, overcoming her previous hostility, invites him to view her wardrobe and seeks his opinion on its contents. But more seems to be at stake here; how else to explain the vehemency of her reactions, what the critic Richard Sheppard called her "disproportionate response"? The landlady is so irked by K's remarks – at one point overcome by a cold shudder – that we might be tempted to agree with W. Emrich (another critic) that the reason she keeps changing her clothes and acquiring new ones is that she has "no firm mental or spiritual substance". She reacts as if to an intrusion on her most personal intimacies: as if K is commenting not on her outerwear but on what lies under it – the successive layers of underclothes, the unclothed body itself and, beneath that, most inaccessible of all, the person, the individual that she is. This reading seems more suggestive than the allegorical one taken by Sheppard, who interprets her clothes as representing the outmoded and threadbare clothing of the Castle institutions, so that in criticising her clothes K is criticising the Castle itself. If this were so, it would be a much less satisfactory image than that of the ladies' handkerchiefs discussed above, having neither the virtue of synecdoche nor the logic which results from integration into the plot. Many Kafka critics seem to lack humility in the face of this multivalency: they prefer the 'either/or' reading where 'both/and' might be more suitable. In *The Castle* we see two contradictory (or complementary?) uses of clothes – on the one hand as the only superficial aspect of appearance upon which all can agree, on the other as the only true indication of someone's nature in a world of baffling appearances – which emphatically reaffirm that equivocal relationship between clothes and bodies first problematized in the 'Clothes' piece of 1908.

Note. Since I first put down these random thoughts years ago, a book has appeared on precisely this subject: Mark M. Anderson, *Kafka's Clothes: Ornament and Aestheticism in the Habsburg Fin de Siècle* (OUP). Anderson's starting point was the same as mine, the observation that this supposedly most 'alienated' of writers took a keen interest in clothes, and women's fashion in particular. Borne aloft on the wings of New Historicism, Anderson takes the argument off into the realms of *Jugendstil* aesthetics, Otto Weininger's 'egoless' woman, the Viennese critique of architectural ornament, the clothing reform movement, nudism, criminology and anti-semitism. In contrast to my own meagre, ahistorical, text-limited survey, it is deeply impressive stuff. But poor Franz has already died a thousand deaths at the hands of his (over-)interpreters, and I worry that Anderson may have added to their number.

Franziska zu Reventlow

Her dates are exactly those of Bismarck's Reich, and her life was one long protest against it. Countess Franziska ('Fanny') zu Reventlow was born in Husum in northern Germany in 1871 and died in Locarno in 1918. Born into a conservative and aristocratic family – her sister became a nun and two of her brothers were members of the German Parliament – she waged a fierce struggle against her parents throughout her adolescence. The first intellectual scene of this rebellion was her secret visits to the Lübeck Ibsen Club, where she encountered free thinkers who propounded artistic and sexual liberation. On her twenty-first birthday she finally ran away from home and her strange quest for self-fulfilment began in earnest. She danced at Carnival in a Pierrot costume. She paid house calls, whip in hand, as a dominatrix. She took acting lessons and played soubrette parts; more strikingly, she appeared as a rope dancer at south German country fairs. All the time she dreamed of a circus life, envying Frank Wedekind his attachment to the Herzog Circus.

After moving to Munich, then artistic capital of Germany, she tried to become a painter, but in fact supported herself by writing, first translations from the French, then satirical sketches, and finally novels. A brief marriage to a Hamburg assessor ended in divorce – her outrageous behaviour, he said, was ruining his career and good name – and disinheritance by her family. The birth in 1897 of her illegitimate son Rolf (she kept his father's identity secret, saying she had given herself the child) caused chronic gynaecological problems but did not slow her erotic or literary schedule. Determined to save him from the German schools system, she educated him at home.

For the next fifteen years she was a central figure in Schwabing, then as now Munich's bohemian quarter, and acted out the ideas which were common currency in its cafes – defiance of bourgeois convention and promotion of sexual freedom. In particular, she embodied the newly fashionable cult of *Mutterrecht*, the belief that there had been an older and better civilisation based on women's rights, women's religion and women-centred families. Her lovers were many: though constantly broke, she always managed to get rich men to pay her way to such places as Constantinople and Corfu. Her circle of acquaintance was huge: in addition to Wedekind (whose 1912 play *Franziska* is loosely based on her career), it included Rainer Maria Rilke ("every morning a poem in my letterbox," she noted with pleasure) and Max Weber (through whose intercession she contrived to have her son exempted from military service).

In 1906, at the home of Otto Gross the maverick psychoanalyst, she met Frieda Weekley, the later Frieda Lawrence, who thought she "had the face of a very young Madonna". Reventlow is thus one of the conduits by which the philosophy of Schwabing penetrates English literature: D.H. Lawrence portrays her in *Mr Noon*. When she left Schwabing for the artists' colony of Ascona in 1910, it was to enter into a farcical marriage for money with a Russian baron – an erstwhile pirate, so he claimed – whose family would only release his inheritance on the condition that he married an aristocrat. No sooner had the newly-weds divided their spoils than they lost it all in a bank collapse.

She died as she had so often lived – penniless.

Reventlow was not a political feminist. Distancing herself from the women's movement in an essay of 1899 ('Viragines or Hetaerae'), she defined herself as a 'hetaera' (roughly speaking, a 'free woman'). She wanted women to have control of their bodies, which she had fought for in her own life. Financial independence interested her less. But in her writings, as in her life, she experimented with alternative ways of living both within and outside the patriarchal society of the Wilhelmine era.

Almost none of her work is available in English.[6] Perhaps it should be? Candidates for translation include the clearly autobiographical novel *Ellen Olestjerne*, the anarchic comic fiction *The Money Complex* (filmed in 2015 by Spanish director Juan Rodrigáñez) and the set of 'amouresques' *From Paul to Pedro*, as well as the wide-ranging *Letters* and *Diaries*.

---

[6] I'm only aware of a short-story collection, *The Guesthouse at the Sign of the Teetering Globe*, tr. James J. Conway (2017).

Rilke and Cézanne

He turned to nature and knew how to swallow back his love for every apple and put it to rest in the painted apple forever. Can you imagine what that is like, and what it's like to experience this through him? I've received the first proofs from the Insel Verlag. In the poems, there are instinctive beginnings towards a similar objectivity. I'm leaving 'The Gazelle' as it is: it's good.

These words were written in Paris on 13 October 1907 by the poet Rainer Maria Rilke. A week earlier he had made his first visit to the retrospective exhibition of Cézanne's paintings at the Salon d'Automne, and in a series of letters to his wife over the next month he reported, on an almost daily basis, his return visits to the exhibition and the exhilaration of his encounters and re-encounters with the painter's work. The weekend of 12/13 October also saw an important event in Rilke's life as a writer: the arrival of the proofs of his latest volume, entitled *New Poems*. These are the poems he had been rereading between visits to the Salon, the poems which, in his view, reached tentatively for the objectivity of which Cézanne was master. My purpose here is to test the validity of that proposition by comparing the aesthetic principles enunciated in the letters with the poetic practice in a select few of the *New Poems*.

The connection was made by others, even while the exhibition was still in progress. On 7 October Rilke met by chance in the Cézanne room the distinguished art patron Count Harry Kessler, who ingratiated himself with the poet by making some flattering remarks about the latter's recently published *Book of Images* (the extended edition, presumably, of 1906). On 18 October Rilke replied enthusiastically to a letter in which Clara, his wife, had compared his "blue pages" (the *New Poems* were written on blue paper) to his reported experience of Cézanne.

Since Rilke normally dated his manuscripts, one way to proceed might be to look for those poems written under the direct influence of the exhibition or shortly after it. However, we find no poems datable to October 1907. A couple, 'Pink Hydrangea' and 'The Flamingos', are dated to autumn 1907 or spring 1908 – these appeared in the second volume of the work, published in 1908 – but the poem which Rilke quoted in the context of "objectivity", 'The Gazelle', was written in July 1907, three months before the Cézanne exhibition opened. Indeed, most of the poems we shall be quoting – 'The Dog', 'The Ball', 'The Mountain' – result from a tremendous surge of energy following Rilke's return to Paris in June of that year after a ten-month absence. Thus the revelation he felt in the face of Cézanne's paintings appeared more by way of a vindication of a truth already intuited. As he wrote to Clara on 18 October:

What you are now saying and affectionately confirming for me is something I had somehow suspected, although I would not have been able to say how far I had developed in the direction corresponding to the immense progress Cézanne achieved in his paintings.

This same letter seeks to define the development which had taken place in the poet. It is a development in *perception*: he now stands "more looking" (*"schauender"*) in front of pictures which previously he would have passed by "with momentary sympathy". But it was not so much the brushwork that engaged his attention, "it was the turning point in these paintings that I recognised, because I had just reached it in my own work". "Turning point" (*"Wendung"*) is a critical word for Rilke. It is the title of a much later poem:

Work of the eyes is done, now
go and do heart-work
on all the images imprisoned within you; for you
overpowered them: but even now you don't know them.[7]

Here is described that active contemplation by which things or places can be assimilated or transformed. It is the same process described earlier in the Cézanne letters. On 9 October Rilke wrote of the two-fold nature of perception in Cézanne, first the "looking and confident receiving" of the object, then the "appropriating and making personal use of what has been received". These two procedures immediately start opposing each other, arguing out loud, "perhaps as a result of becoming conscious". This last phrase is significant, for it is the first mention of an idea developed much more fully on 21 October, that "ideally a painter (and, generally, an artist) should not become conscious of his insights"; they should arrive "without taking the detour through his reflective processes". Perception should be unconscious; or, rather, it should take place at a level of consciousness no higher than that of a dog. Van Gogh's anguished self-portrait, he remarks in an earlier letter, "looks shabby and tormented, almost desperate, but not devastated: the way a dog looks when it's in a bad way". Visiting the Cézanne room on 12 October with the painter Mathilde Vollmoeller – to get a second opinion on his own diagnosis, as it were – Rilke was delighted when she remarked: "He sat there in front of [his subject] like a dog, just looking, without any nervousness, without any ulterior

---

[7] Tr. Stephen Mitchell

motive". Delighted, because this was precisely how Rilke characterised Cézanne's perception in his own self-portrait. The painter regarded himself "with the faith and the sympathetic yet objective interest of a dog that sees itself in the mirror and thinks: there's another dog" (letter of 23 October).

These canine references can be of assistance when considering the poem 'The Dog'. It finds in the dog an analogy for the artist's peripheral social situation and his perception of a world which his glances are always re-establishing as true but which it is difficult to represent and even harder to grasp: "Unsure, he gives the image his reality / and then, forgetting, none the less / holds up his face to it beseechingly…"[8]

This brings us to the second stage of the process as described in the letter of 9 October. Having looked and taken over the object of perception, the artist must then make it his own. In an ecstatic description of the portrait of Madame Cézanne on 21 October, Rilke explains that the artist had so perfectly translated the object into its painterly equivalents that its "bourgeois reality" yields up all heaviness to arrive at "a final and definitive picture-existence" where everything is "settled among the colours themselves". This is the achievement that Rilke had hoped to emulate in the *New Poems*. 'The Gazelle', we recall, might exemplify its instinctive beginnings. This poem forms part of a series on animal subjects. In the published volume, it is preceded by 'The Panther' (inspired by a creature seen in the Jardin des Plantes) and followed by a mythical beast, 'The Unicorn'. Thus the sequence represents a migration from a real zoological garden to a mythological *hortus conclusus*. Suspended between the two, the gazelle enacts

---

[8] Tr. Stephen Cohn

the process of representation by which the real object is transformed into the art object:

Enchanted one: how shall the harmony
of two perfect words attain that rhyme
which ripples through you like a spell?[9]

The gazelle's name struggles to attain a rhyme, yet it is endowed with leaf and lyre, the attributes of Apollo, god of poetry. Rilke had watched real gazelles, but under the transforming power of imagination, "it was as if only now, for the first time, they underwent this transmutation" (letter of 13 June 1907). They became something else. In the poem they become punningly assimilated to the 'ghazal', the Persian and Arabic verse form for amatory and bacchanalian themes. The transferability of technique from one art form to another is taken for granted; Horace's axiom *"ut pictura poesis"* ("as is painting so is poetry") applies. In his letter of 15 October, when Rilke is seeking to describe the Cambodian dancers who so fascinated Rodin that he followed them on tour, he first likens them to "transformed gazelles", but then at once switches the image to the realm of sculpture: they have torsos "as if made of a single piece, long hammered out". At the same time he is at pains to point out the limitations of words. They are happiest, Rilke says, when used for descriptive purposes:

...and the words, which feel so unhappy when made to denote purely painterly facts, are only too eager to return to themselves in the description of the man portrayed [in Cézanne's self-portrait], for here's where their proper domain begins. (23 October)

---

[9] Tr. Edward Snow

On the previous day he had lamented the impossibility of describing the portrait of Madame Cézanne – "my blood describes it within me, but the naming of it passes by somewhere outside and is not called in" – and then spends several hundred words describing it!

All these difficulties found utterance at approximately the same time in 'The Flamingos', which can be read as a poem about representation:

In these Fragonard-like mirrorings
no more of their white and pink
is proffered than if a man
said of his mistress: "So soft
she was with sleep."...[10]

"*In Spiegelbildern wie von Fragonard…*" Whether art mirrors life or life mirrors art, by no process of mimesis can visual or verbal representation do justice to reality. The art-historical reference in line 1, to Fragonard, a specialist in erotic subjects, is matched in line 8 by an allusion to the courtesan who is supposed to have been the model for Praxiteles' Venus, a sculpture which has not survived: the one an unattainable mirror image, the other an ir-recoverable lost image. Yet the flamingos behave "*more* seductively than Phryne". She is the standard of comparison and the verbal simile for the birds' self-reflexive absorption. Rilke demonstrates himself, probably with intention, at a loss for words and, in the last line, has the birds step one by one "into the imaginary". Quite where this might be is uncertain. Into the poem, perhaps, or out of the poem, away from the confinement of language represented by the aviary with its envious screeches and to a place where "the naming of it passes by somewhere outside".

---

[10] Tr. Galway Kinnell and Hannah Liebmann

In his letter of 13 October Rilke identifies "objectivity" as the essence of Cézanne's art, to which he aspired in poetry. The same letter offers a definition of the term. "Objectivity" requires that the artist does not show the love he feels for the object of representation; it is necessary to "go beyond love". Otherwise, "one judges it instead of saying it", and that way lies the peril of "mood painting" ("*Stimmungsmalerei*"). An exactly analogous danger exists for the poet. Before the clarification of vision achieved by exposure to Cézanne – and, earlier, Rodin – Rilke had himself regarded Nature as "a general occasion… I was not yet sitting before her; I allowed myself to be swept away by the soul that was emanating from her". A few months after the exhibition closed he was to summarise the advantages of "saying" over "judging" in the 'Requiem' for Wolf von Kalckreuth, a poet of promise who had taken his own life at the age of only nineteen:

O ancient curse of poets!
Being sorry for themselves instead of saying,
For ever passing judgement on their feeling
instead of shaping it; for ever thinking
that what is sad or joyful in themselves
is what they know and what in poems may fitly
be mourned or celebrated. Invalids,
using a language full of woefulness
to tell us where it hurts, instead of sternly
transmuting into words those selves of theirs,
as imperturbable cathedral carvers
transposed themselves into the constant stone.[11]

The poet, then, should be like a stonemason, working in a material as implacable and indifferent as stone. Cézanne's

---

[11] Tr. J. B. Leishman

pictorial representation was of the same order. His paintings present facts and

their fairest judge would surely be the one who could quietly confirm them in their existence without experiencing anything in them anything more or other than facts. (18 October)

The German word *"Sache"* ("matter", "things") is implicated in both the word for "fact" (*"Tatsache"*) and the word usually translated as "objectivity" (*"Sachlichkeit"*). It is his uncompromising objectivity which makes Cézanne's portraits appear offensive to many, so Rilke continues in the letter of 18 October. Like Baudelaire – an idol for Rilke and his fictional *alter ego* Malte Laurids Brigge alike – Cézanne realised that "even something horrible, something that seems no more than disgusting, *is*, and shares the truth of its being with everything else that exists" (19 October). All things have equal beauty under the transforming power of art; Baudelaire taught how the artist must be prepared to lie down with the leper.

Objectivity carries with it an obligation to the object. *"La réalisation"*, Cézanne called it; in Rilke's vocabulary "the conviction of becoming a thing" (9 October). Of the fruit in a still life the poet writes: "In Cézanne they cease to be edible altogether, so very thing-like (*dinghaft*) and real they have become, so simply indestructible in their stubborn there-ness" (8 October). The concept of the "thing" (*"Ding"*) has been much discussed. Many critics have referred to a proportion of the *New Poems* as "thing-poems". The idea originates with Rilke's monograph on Rodin (the poet worked for a while as the sculptor's secretary). A "thing" is self-contained, "in a complete state of self-concern". It is surrounded by silence and space but it translates dynamic energy into visual volume. It is a spatialisation of time. A "thing" is not any object but a constructively created one, an embodiment of abstraction, of thought, of human handiwork. Such an object is evoked in 'The Ball'. This poem Rilke (reportedly) considered his best because in it he had articulated "nothing but the almost inexpressible sense of a pure movement". The ball is "too little thing, yet still thing enough". The poet has reduced it to its two or three essential qualities: its ability to be thrown, its upward flight, its downward flight. In the opening lines the ball, its abstract quality made concrete – "you round [one]" – is released from warm hands to begin its flight. Halfway through the poem, at the highest point of its trajectory, it pauses for a moment, defying gravity, and is again apostrophised: "you, between fall and flight still un-decided". Finally – displaying the art beyond art which Rilke appreciated in Cézanne's still life, "simply, artlessly" – it falls into the receiving cup of outstretched hands.

At times a "thing" can acquire the status of a holy relic. On 9 October Rilke described how Cézanne would arrange fruit and wine bottles prior to painting them "and (like Van Gogh) he makes his 'saints' out of such things; and forces them, *forces* them, to be beautiful". The following day he remarks that the miracle of artistic making can be valid "only for one person, every time; only for the saint to whom it happens" – an idea previously expressed in several of the *New Poems*. For example, in 'The Unicorn' a figure called "the saint" is surprised by "the never-believed", a creature of the human imagination in the image of a beast. Since this poem was inspired by a tapestry, 'Dame à la Licorne', it is intriguing to note that Rilke changed the human participant from a virgin (or the Virgin), to whom unicorns traditionally appeared, to a masculine '*Heiliger*'. In 'The Donor' the apparition, this time of the Saviour, also appears uniquely and unexpectedly to the observer and is "deep in its own concerns and self-immersed", a phrase reminiscent of the Rodin monograph.

A year after his Cézanne epiphany, Rilke brought together notions of perception, representation and canonisation in three tender lines from a poem commemorating Paula Modersohn-Becker, the painter who had taught him so much about art at the Worpswede Artists' Colony when he stayed there between 1900 and 1902:

So free of curiosity your gaze had become,
so unpossessive, of such true poverty
that it no longer desired your self: holy.

What Modersohn-Becker had particularly to impart was an eye for colour, and colour was the single greatest revelation for Rilke in Cézanne. On 8 October he reflected that he could imagine someone writing a monograph on the colour blue – "what a biography!" From his lyrical evocation of the distinctive eighteenth-century blue of La Tour and Perronneau and the dense waxy blue of the Pompeiian wall paintings, one might suppose Rilke uniquely qualified for the task, so passionately does he write of Cézanne's colours: how the painter recognises one colour beneath another; where we see only grey "he doesn't relent and pulls out all the violet hues that had been tucked inside, as it were" (24 October). And how painting is nothing but an "intercourse" among colours (21 October). The following day he seeks to define this last point more exactly, and as if set off by the human and animal associations of the word "intercourse" he reaches, as frequently in these letters, for the image of the dog:

Just as in the mouth of a dog various secretions will gather in anticipation of the approach of various things – consenting ones for drawing out nutrients, and correcting ones to neutralise poisons: in the same way, various intensifications and dilutions take place in the core of every colour, helping it to survive contact with others.

In Cézanne's earlier (Paris) period, Rilke suggests, colour was merely an end in itself. Later, he used it personally, as no one had used colour before, "simply for making the object" (12 October). He sought an exact colour equivalent of the object portrayed, much as if, in the simile suggested to Rilke by Mathilde Vollmoeller, he had a pair of scales and placed the object on one side, the colour on the other. It is tempting to see Rilke's poetic practice as an analogous process. In the 1950s the critic Hans Berendt took several passages from the letters and, by substituting "word" for "colour", believed that he had arrived at an "almost technically exact description" of what Rilke was doing. Several poems in the collection are articulations of colour and provide a convenient test case for this proposition. 'Blue Hydrangea' is one such:

These leaves are like the last green
in the paint pots—dried up, dull, and rough,
behind the flowered umbels whose blue
is not their own, only mirrored from far away.[12]

Here is the process of unpacking a colour, much as Cézanne revealed violet beneath the grey: in the "old blue letters" – perhaps recalling the blue manuscript on which Rilke's poems were first inscribed – are undertones of yellow, violet and grey. The poem opens allusively (and elusively) by comparing a natural blue, that of the hydrangea (or the sky reflected in a hydrangea), to a painter's green. In the final

---

[12] Tr. Rick Barot

stanza an active intercourse between colours is evoked with the sight of a "touching blue" rejoicing beside the green. In a letter of 22 October, the red armchair on which Madame Cézanne sat is described as containing within itself "an experienced sum of colour", much as the hydrangea's blue seems to encompass a personal history, the history of some love affair recorded on old blue letter paper. And in line 2 the post-positioned adjectives, "dried up, dull and rough", have the effect of shifting emphasis to the characteristics of the objects, as if searching for their exact equivalents in words.

'Blue Hydrangea' was written in July 1906. In a related poem, composed much closer in time to the Cézanne letters, 'Pink Hydrangea' (autumn 1907/spring 1908), the tone is different:

Who would suppose this pink? And who knew
that it was gathering in these umbels?
Like golden things that lose their gilt,
They gently unredden, as if from use.

Yet they demand nothing for such pink!
Does it stay for them, smiling from on high?
Are angels there, to catch it tenderly
When, generous as scent, it fades?

Or perhaps again they give it up
so that it never feels a withering.
But under this pink a green
has listened and now wilts, all-knowing.

Here colour is translated to a metaphysical realm, so that it might never experience withering. The colour green has knowledge of transience, but pink remains unconscious. Pink is a chromatic ambiguity, poised between red and white, and Rilke announces it by way of a *verbal* ambiguity in the German original: *"Wer nahm das Rosa an?"* What does this question mean? Who assumed the pink? Who accepted it? Who took it on? Thus the poem enacts in words the artist's method in paint. Perhaps not the very best method, however, for the last two lines echo a passage in the letter of 21 October where Rilke draws unfavourable comparison between Van Gogh and Cézanne. Van Gogh, on the evidence of his published letters, is held up as the inferior artist because he was self-conscious. He knew "that blue called for orange and green for red: that, secretly, listening in his eye's interior, he had heard such things spoken, the inquisitive one". The green of the poem has this same debilitating awareness and its penalty is to wither. It, too, has "listened" (but note that the ambiguity of the first line is imitated in the last, since *"gehorcht"* in the original can mean both "listened" and "obeyed"). The artist who lies in wait for his perceptions, instead of waiting to be taken by them unawares, will find them transformed for the worse, "like the beautiful gold in the fairy tale which cannot remain gold because some small detail was not taken care of". The umbels of the hydrangea suffer this fate, gently un-burdening themselves of their attribute of pinkness "like golden things that lose their gilt". In both cases, reverse alchemy provides an image of unachieved art, of something which, at worst, leads to "pure intentionality, pure high-handedness – in short, to decoration" (letter of 21 October).

In one further respect, beyond his uncluttered perceptions and unawareness of his own insights, Cézanne suggested an ideal of the artist – in his dedication to work. As Rilke noted on 9 October, this is the man who was too busy to attend his mother's funeral because he was engaged *"sur le motif"*. We would only have to look at his hands to know "how massively and genuinely the work lay in them right to the end" (18 October). Under his inspiration Rilke feels himself "on the way to becoming a worker" (13 October), but all the time he is held back by the seductiveness of idleness by comforting memories of times spent without working, "memories of lying still and taking comfort" (4 October). Cézanne, by contrast, would trudge every day to his studio, followed by the mockery of children and a hail of stones as if he were a stray dog (8 October). Here again we find a portrait of the artist as an old dog. In the following letter, work is personified as the dog *owner*, an arbitrary master who calls him, beats him, lets him starve, allowing him off the leash only on Sundays to return to his lifelong pieties "as if to his original owner". The poem 'The Dog' again comes to mind. Work is an "incomprehensible master" (*"unbegreiflicher Herr"*) for Cézanne (9 October); in the poem's last stanza the dog is "almost understanding, close to approval" (*"beinah begreifend, nah am Einverstehen"*). No amount of effort expended on the artwork will ever achieve that approval, as is made apparent in another poem, 'The Mountain':

Thirty-six and then a hundred times
the printmaker inscribed that mountain, torn
away and always driven back again
(thirty-six and then a hundred times)
to the inscrutable volcano...[13]

The poem makes explicit what was only to be inferred in other poems: *ut pictura poesis*; the painter *writes* the mountain. But however many times the obsessive, workaholic Hokusai "writes" and rewrites Mount Fuji, the volcano remains stubbornly "incomprehensible" (*"unbegreiflich"*), refusing to accommodate itself to the artist's

---

[13] Tr. Susan McLean

outline or set a limit to its "magnificence" ("*Herrlichkeit*" – from the root "*Herr*"). The third stanza enacts, instead, Fujiyama's eruption, both volcanic and perceptual, in a cascade of present participles: "emerging", "allowing", "consuming", "knowing".

Rilke was quite modest about his achievements as art historian. He was only capable, he wrote on 15 October, of "a provisional, personal insight". What prompted this remark was a re-encounter with some drawings by his old master Rodin. Viewing them again after a passage of time, he was disappointed by their interpretability; he would have preferred them "without any accent, more discreet, more factual, left alone with themselves". The suspicion expressed here is entirely consistent with what he wrote in other letters about intention and self-awareness. Rilke later evolved an idea that the poem on the page should reproduce the laborious thought-processes of its author: the unfinished quality of the *Duino Elegies* (1912-22) is, in this sense, the antithesis of Classicism. But at the period of the *New Poems* his concern was much more to achieve, by a heroic routine of hard work, an exact equilibrium between descriptor and described. We have confirmed that that the *Letters on Cézanne* offer a retrospective summation of many of Rilke's practices in the poems, but what is less certain is that he himself saw any connection beyond "instinctive beginnings". Of the crucial letter of 13 October in which this phrase occurs, K. A. J. Batterby wrote: "Rilke was now rationally conscious of the underlying principle involved; he could now grasp it and examine it with his intelligence" (*Rilke and France*, 1966). It is debatable whether Rilke possessed "intelligence" as the word is used here. He was gifted in abundance with that quality of selfless receptivity Keats called "negative capability" and it is this which directed his poetic practice more than "intelligence". A sharper insight comes from Michael Hamburger, one of his most sensitive translators, who said of Rilke:

No other poet of his time had so fluid a personality, so wide a range of masks and styles; but also of sympathies and attitudes which exclude and contradict one another as soon as we look at them from a pragmatic or logical point of view. (*The Truth of Poetry*, 1972)

From a poet who mistrusted self-awareness in artists, we should not expect systematic thinking, but only its "instinctive beginnings". It is with this tentative formulation that I begin – and end – my attempt to relate letters to poems.

Note. Most of the translations of the letters are taken from *Letters on Cézanne*, tr. Joel Agee (Vintage, 1991). Otherwise, any uncredited translations are my own. The secondary literature on Rilke is vast, the latest contribution being a 656-page *magnum opus* by my old postgrad stablemate Charlie Louth entitled *Rilke: The Life of the Work* (OUP, 2020).

On Translating Poetry

They say you should never meet your heroes. Disillusionment may not be far behind. Someone I always admired was the poet and translator Michael Hamburger (1924-2007). I met him only once, in the late Nineties at the University of East Anglia, where he was giving a seminar on 'Translating Goethe'. His insights were sharp, as you'd expect from someone with his distinguished record of publication. But mostly I retain an impression of *bitterness*. As he drew on his cigarette and chatted with me (amiably enough), I thought, *This man is seriously pissed off with how the world has treated him*. Perhaps I read him wrong? Still, it is a fact that the literary translator is often undervalued. He presents himself at the imposing door of the House of Literature, only to be met by a rather snooty butler who looks him up and down and says, "Tradesmen's entrance is round the back."[14]

No area of translation presents as many challenges as the translation of poetry, the field that Hamburger made his own. In the past I've struggled – and failed – with

---

[14] When foreign drama is presented in new translation, it's common practice to bury the translator's name way down the credits, giving the impression that the script is the sole work of whichever box-office name has been attached to the project. I feel relieved that when my own translation of Wedekind's *Franziska* was used as the basis for a London production, the director (Georgina Van Welie) insisted on including my name under that of the adapter (the poet Eleanor Brown) on the publicity and published text.

Hofmannsthal. More recently I've struggled – and probably failed – with Rainer Maria Rilke. Rilke wrote to Countess Sizzo in March 1922 that each word in a poem is semantically unique. He insisted that this applied to the most banal and everyday parts of speech (such as conjunctions or the definite article) and that it divided a poem from all current usage inside its own vernacular. Such a position, if followed through, would make any translation of verse, other than the clumsiest literalism, futile. (I'm not sure how far Rilke himself followed it through – he 'translated' poems from French and English into his own heightened, idiosyncratic German.)

Reviewing Edward Snow's translations of Rilke in the *New York Times*, the poet and translator Michael Hofmann concluded: "Of course, these poems are impossible." Hofmann drew attention to the last line of a crucial eight-line one called 'Narcissus' which runs: "*und hob sich auf und konnte nicht mehr sein*" ["and annulled himself and could exist no more."] Here Rilke is playing in perhaps five or six ways with the German verb *aufheben*, meaning variously to preserve, lift up or abolish. This example struck home with me, since I once attempted a musical setting of this very Rilke poem, using my own provisional English translation as the basis for a text. I say "provisional" because I found myself bending the translation as I went along in order to accommodate words to my preferred musical line. In his heavyweight study of translation, *After Babel*, George Steiner devotes several pages to demonstrating how the musical setting of poetry is yet another form of 'translation', remarking how even masterly *Lieder* composers like Schumann and Schubert were inclined to alter their source text when the poet's words didn't 'fit' their music.

Some assert that translation should be a two-person job:

one to translate *out of* the source language, the other to translate *into* the target language. It's debatable how many people are 100 per cent bilingual. Such a person might discharge both functions with distinction. For the rest of us, who may juggle a 'mother tongue' with one or more acquired foreign languages, translation will always expose our blind spots, our sheer ignorance of context or local nuance. Early in 1949, the BBC radio producer Archie Harding proposed the commissioning of a new translation of Goethe's *Faust* to mark the 200th anniversary of Goethe's birth in August 1749. He approached W.H. Auden, who had good German, but Auden declined. Harding then turned to his BBC colleague, the poet Louis MacNeice. MacNeice was reluctant at first, claiming that he had "next to no German" (unusual, one would have thought, in a classicist of his generation) and, besides, was "somewhat prejudiced against Goethe". However, he accepted the job, on the condition that his old friend Ernst Stahl, then Reader in German at Oxford, could work with him. Stahl provided him with a literal translation and, over the course of several months' collaboration, the two men decided where the cuts in this 12,000-line work should be made to accommodate it within six programmes, before MacNeice began trans-muting German poetry into his own English verse. Stahl later reflected that his friend's lack of bilingual knowledge was a positive advantage: MacNeice was guided only by the literal rendering before him and his own intuition. He refused to look at Shelley's or any other English versions. As MacNeice's biographer, Jon Stallworthy, observes, the poet showed "particular ingenuity in adapting Goethe's many and varied verse forms: blank verse, free verse, two-beat lines, hexameters, trimeters, tetrameters, choric odes and alexandrines." It was a monumental achievement, recreating not only Goethe's prosody and rhyme schemes but also (as MacNeice put it himself) "a variation of mood and modulation of diction corresponding to Goethe's own". The famous final lines of the verse-drama may serve as illustration. Goethe has:

Alles Vergängliche
Ist nur ein Gleichnis;
Das Unzulängliche,
Hier wird's Ereignis;
Das Unbeschreibliche,
Hier ist's getan;
Das Ewig-Weibliche
Zieht uns hinan.

MacNeice renders this as:

All that is past of us
Was but reflected;
All that was lost in us
Here is corrected;
All indescribables
Here we descry;
Eternal Womanhead
Leads us on high.

Compare a standard 'free-verse' translation:

All things transitory
are but parable;
here insufficiency
becomes fulfilment,
here the indescribable
is accomplished;
the ever-womanly
draws us heavenward.
(tr. Friedel Becker/Peggie Cochrane)

MacNeice heroically imitates the original rhyme scheme, although he is stumped as any translator would be by *unbeschreiblich/weiblich*. The Becker/Cochrane version is closer to the literal 'meaning' of the words, but having forfeited the metre and rhyme of the original, is theirs a trade-off we are prepared to accept? Perhaps, just as MacNeice's *Faust* was a two-man job, so we could think of reading translated poetry as a multi-text activity: assemble a range of versions, one that purports to translate the words, another that prioritises imitating the prosody of the original, one by a scholar, one by a poet... Not necessarily an "impossible" task, *pace* Michael Hofmann, just a very exacting one.

Three Poems by Hofmannsthal

Mindful of my strictures and anxieties about translating verse, I shyly resurrect these clumsy efforts from the 1990s to English three early poems by Hugo von Hofmannsthal (1874-1929) written a century earlier. If memory serves, the occasion was the possible publication by Carcanet Press of a volume of Hofmannsthal's verse. Michael Schmidt, Carcanet's editorial director, was unimpressed by my locutions, rightly suspecting that Michael Hamburger would have done it so much better. The poems are 'Manche freilich…' (1895), 'Die Beiden' (1896) and 'Über Vergänglichkeit' (1894).

SOME THERE ARE…

Some there are who must perish below,
Where the weighty oars of the galleys scour,
Others dwell aloft by the helm,
Know the flight of birds and the resort of stars.

Some will always lie with heavy limbs
Among the roots of tangled life,
While for others places are set
With the sibyls, the empresses,
And there they will sit as if at home,
Light heads on lighter shoulders.

But a shadow falls from those lives
Across into the other lives,

And the light are bound to the heavy
As the air and earth are bound:

Weariness of quite-forgotten peoples
I cannot dismiss from my eyelids,
Nor ward off from my terrified soul
The silent fall of distant stars.

Many fates are woven next to mine,
Existence merges all of them in play,
And my part is more than this life's
Slender flame or narrow lyre.

THE COUPLE

She held the goblet in one hand
-- Her mouth and chin were like its rim --
So light and certain was her gait
No droplet from the glass escaped.

So light and firm was his command:
He rode upon a sprightly horse,
And with a single careless gesture
Brought it, quivering, to a stop.

And yet, when it was time for him
To take the dainty vessel from her,
Its weight defied their joint attempt:

For both of them were trembling so
That neither found the other's hand
And ruby wine spilt on the ground.

ON TRANSITORINESS

Upon my cheeks I feel still their breath:
How can it be that these so recent days
Are gone, gone for ever, as if in death?

This is a thing that no one fully knows,
Beyond lament, too dreadful to erase:
That everything glides by us, ebbs and flows.

And that my own self, quite unbound, appeared
Gliding out from a little child and rose
Towards me silent, like a dog, and weird.

A hundred years ago I too was there
And my forebears, asleep in shrouds, are near
To me, akin as I to my own hair,

As one with me as I with my own hair.

Hofmannsthals in Exile

Several years ago I had the pleasure of meeting Octavian von Hofmannsthal. An affable gent, somewhat older than myself, he was a living link to a part of my own past. For Octavian is the grandson of Hugo von Hofmannsthal, the Austrian poet and dramatist whose voluminous literary output was the subject of my doctorate at Cambridge. I'd approached the grandson having become interested in what happened to the family after Hugo's premature death in 1929. I knew some of it. Over drinks in the Chelsea Arts Club, Octavian helped to fill out the story.

As the storm clouds gathered in the 1930s, emigration was a pressing concern in view of the family's Jewish ancestry. The family property was seized by the Nazis in 1938. Gerty von Hofmannsthal, the widow, moved to England in July 1939, where she joined a substantial *émigré* community in Oxford, some of them people she had already known in Vienna – people like Heinz Cassirer (later to be Iris Murdoch's philosophy tutor), the young poet Michael Hamburger, the anthropologist Franz Baermann Steiner and the composer and musicologist Egon Wellesz (of whom more below).

Hugo and Gerty had two surviving children, Christiane and Raimund (another son, Franz, took his own life, a tragedy that seems to have hastened Hugo's own end). Christiane married a Sanskrit scholar, Heinrich Zimmer, and emigrated to the USA in 1940. Initially active as a social worker in New York, she rose to become an assistant professor at Fordham University. Raimund, both deep-rootedly Viennese and a lifelong anglophile with an easy social manner, had little trouble integrating into his adopted culture, even if those close to him grow vague when asked to define his achievement. To John Julius Norwich "it was a genius for friendship, and for the spontaneous, infectious enjoyment of all the beauties and blessings life had to offer, great and small". Isaiah Berlin, writing his obituary in 1974, was no more specific:

Raimund was not himself a creative artist, but he venerated art and artists, particularly musicians, beyond other men. His view of society was of a piece with this: he saw human beings in aesthetic and emotional terms – Society, the great world, was, to him, a stage, a pageant, a dream or a nightmare, but seldom a realistic spectacle of humdrum, everyday life. (*The Times*, 26 April 1974)

For more than thirty years, according to a colleague, he performed an "amorphous but invaluable" role with the *Time-Life* organisation as "ambassador, scout, mender of fences, social mentor and guide, interpreter". He had first joined *Time*'s London office in 1938, then moved in 1940 to America, where he took US citizenship, before returning to Europe as a private with the US Army. He ended his career as European Director of Time Books and Arts Associates.

Raimund married twice. His first wife was the heiress Alice Astor – daughter of John Jacob Astor IV, one of the victims of the *Titanic* disaster. He remarried in 1939. His second bride (Octavian's mother) was top-drawer English aristocracy: Elizabeth Paget, daughter of the Marquess of Anglesey and niece to Lady Diana Cooper. Dark-haired, blue-eyed with "creamy, magnolia skin" and variously described as "one of the most beautiful women in London" or "the most beautiful girl in England", Liz must have been quite a catch. As a couple they flit across the social scene of the war years. Evelyn Waugh was a friend, although as ever with Waugh friendship was no protection from a waspish tongue:

On the Saturday I ate oysters with Raimund von Hofmannsthal and returned with him to lunch with Liz, lovely but seldom in the room…. On Tuesday Liz lunched with me at Wilton's, ate nothing, looked ill and nervous, and when later Raimund joined us seemed overcome with aversion. He, too, discomposed and morose. Perhaps a climax of some kind in their lives. (E. Waugh, *Diaries*, 4 May 1944)

Octavian was born on 13 February 1946. Visiting a few days later, Waugh showed his customary empathy for a nursing mother: "I called on Liz at her new charming little house in Wilton Street where she returned that day from the nursing home. Dazzling beauty but rather dull." On 8 August he "dined with Liz and Raimund and found her becoming a scold."

A very different impression of the fragrant Elizabeth emerges from Gully Wells's memoir *The House in France*. This lady is anything but "dull". At one time Liz and Wells's mother, Dee, were both competitors for the attentions of A.J. (Freddie) Ayer, priapic exponent of Logical Positivism. Dee confided in a letter to a friend how she wished "somebody would poison that f-ing Lady L. von H. *She* is the biggest fly in anyone's ointment and I think fills F[reddie]'s head with stories of how ruthless and uncivilized I am and will make him miserable." Years later, when Dee had won her man, the two erstwhile rivals became friends, and Gully has an amusing anecdote of visiting the von Hofmannsthals with her mother and taking the opportunity to peep into the medicine cabinet (to "see what interesting pills she might be taking") and raid the dressing table to douse herself with their hostess's perfume.

I'd like to know more about Alice Astor. Raimund was, in fact, her second husband. Her first marriage was to Serge Obolensky, a scion of the Russian Imperial family who pops up in the most unexpected places (I first encountered him as the matchmaker behind novelist Michael Arlen's marriage.) His self-aggrandizing memoirs, *One Man in His Time*, present Alice as seductive if somewhat dotty. Reputedly one of the first four people to enter Tutankhamun's tomb – a claim I have been unable to verify – she was convinced that she was the reincarnation of an Egyptian princess, the daughter of the High Priest of Heliopolis. This was all well before Octavian's time, but he was kind enough to put me in touch with a relative whose grandmother was Gerty's sister and whose mother was Raimund's cousin. This contact produced an unpublished family memoir which rounded out more detail of the Hofmannsthals' life after the *Anschluss*. Here, Alice emerges sympathetically as someone who continued to support the Austrian refugees emotionally and financially even after her divorce from Raimund. Towards the end of her life, after the collapse of her fourth and final marriage, she grew even dottier. She began to experiment with telepathy, spiritualism and extra sensory perception, channelling some of her fortune into supporting the work of maverick psychic researcher Andrija Puharic. At her New York residence in the 1950s she introduced Puharic to Aldous Huxley, by then deeply immersed himself in mysticism and magic mushrooms, and she makes several tantalising appearances in Huxley's published letters.

Egon Wellesz

The composer and musicologist Egon Wellesz was born into an affluent Viennese family of Jewish origins in 1885. His parents, Samu Wellesz and Ilona Lovenyi, were both migrants from the Hungarian parts of the Empire, his father a textile manufacturer, his mother an amateur musician. Egon, their only child, attended the Franz Joseph Gymnasium in Vienna, where he received a thorough classical education, which was later to serve him well. For his thirteenth birthday, 1898, he was taken to the Opera, to hear *Der Freischütz*, conducted by Gustav Mahler, and in his memoirs, published many years later, he recalls this as the decisive experience which determined him to become a composer.

Initially, however, he was destined for the law. In German-speaking countries, to this day, study of law is a prerequisite for entry into the public service. So he enrolled at the law faculty at Vienna University. Meanwhile a friend, knowing of his musical ambitions, alerted him to a couple of teachers in Vienna whose influence would be decisive for his future. One was Guido Adler, Professor of Music History at the University, who nurtured Wellesz's interests in musicology and directed him towards the study of Baroque opera. Adler was a friend of Mahler and contrived to get his students admitted to Mahler's rehearsals. To the end of his life Wellesz was still dining out on his stories of how he sat at Mahler's feet, and showing visitors his scores of Mahler symphonies that he'd annotated during rehearsals. The other great teacher was an impoverished, chain-smoking composer just then returned to Vienna – Arnold Schoenberg. Wellesz took private lessons with him from 1904 to 1906. These were lessons in harmony, counterpoint and fugue, not "composition" – Wellesz always claimed to be self-taught as a composer – but from his early compositions like the *Drei Skizzen* for piano (1911) it's clear that Schoenberg's example as composer was before his eyes, just as Mahler's had been in those orchestral rehearsals he attended.

The young Wellesz moved in progressive circles that included the poet Rilke, the architect Adolf Loos and the painter Kokoschka, whose 1911 portrait of the composer is one of the most familiar images of him. Continuing his studies at the University, where Anton Webern was a friend and fellow student, he took his doctorate in 1908 with a dissertation on Giuseppe Bonno and Baroque opera. The same year he married a childhood friend, Emmy Stross, who was later to achieve distinction as an art historian. Two daughters were born to them in the following years, Magdalena and Elisabeth. Presented with the necessity of making a living, Wellesz ruled out the life of a provincial conductor; and he certainly had no intention of orchestrating third-rate operettas, as the cash-strapped Schoenberg was forced to do. (One of Wellesz's less flattering anecdotes about his teacher concerned Schoenberg's continual requests to borrow money off him). Wellesz chose instead the path of academic musicology, being appointed lecturer in music history at Vienna in 1913. Interested now in the common elements of eastern and western chant, he set himself the problem of deciphering Byzantine musical notation, which no one had yet done. Declared medically unfit for war service, he pursued this ambition through the war years and published his solution in 1918. Here was the foundation of his reputation as a Byzantine scholar, which survives to this day, even among those who have never heard a note of his music.

But his interest in contemporary music was as strong as these scholarly interests. After World War I he joined E.J. Dent and Rudolf Réti to found the International Society for Contemporary Music, which encouraged first performances of French and British composers, as well as the Austrians and Germans. Throughout his years in Vienna, he maintained his links with the Schoenberg circle, publishing the first biography of his teacher in 1921 and taking an active part in Schoenberg's Society for Private Musical Performances, where a number of Wellesz's own early chamber works were first heard. In 1935 Webern organised a fiftieth birthday concert for Wellesz in Vienna. All the time these varied influences, contemporary and historical, were feeding into his own compositions. A first encounter with what he called the "Hellenic clarity" of Debussy's music helped to free him from the debilitating post-Wagnerian legacy of his youth. Diaghilev's Ballets Russes visited Vienna in 1912 and 1913, suggesting to Wellesz new possibilities for stage action, an alternative to the "subjectivity" of Strauss's operas. The first result of this was a ballet, *Das Wunder der Diana* (The Miracle of Diana), to a scenario by Béla Balázs, who was Bartók's collaborator on *The Wooden Prince* and *Duke Bluebeard's Castle*. Between 1914 and 1931 his compositional energies went into writing for the stage: four ballets and five operas, which were performed and well received in Germany and Austria. His collaborators on these projects were some of the more notable artists of the day. *Die Prinzessin Girnara* had a libretto by Jakob Wassermann (a respected novelist). *Die*

Opferung des Gefangenen (The Sacrifice of the Prisoner) was choreographed by Kurt Jooss (another of the "Hitler Emigrés", who ended up in England in the 1940s, at Dartington Hall). Because of his academic commitments, Wellesz was perforce a vacation composer, taking off every summer to the Austrian resort of Altaussee. Here in 1918 he began a friendship with Hugo von Hofmannsthal, best known as Richard Strauss's librettist. Their common interest in Greek myth led to several collaborations: a ballet, *Achilles auf Skyros*, and two of Wellesz's finest works, the operas *Alkestis* and *Die Bakchantinnen* (The Bacchae). The latter, first performed in 1931, was the only one of his operas to be premiered in Vienna, at the State Opera under Clemens Krauss.

So at this point, 1931/1932, we find Wellesz really at the peak of his success. Throughout the 1920s he had enjoyed considerable esteem, especially in Germany, as a composer. He was also active as a music journalist and consolidating his reputation as a scholar. He founded the Byzantine Research Institute at Vienna in 1932 and was appointed Professor of Music History at the University. But, of course, the political storm clouds were gathering. The German opera stage was no longer so welcoming. Around this time Wellesz converted to Catholicism and channelled the hieratic and ritualistic propensities of his recent operas into choral and liturgical works. Also, in the early Thirties, he cemented the ties with Britain which were to prove his salvation later. Oxford University, wishing to mark the bicentenary of Haydn's birth, had looked for a representative living Austrian composer on whom to confer an honorary doctorate; the choice fell on Wellesz. The following year (1933) he was in London, giving a series of guest lectures on opera. He had plans for one further opera of his own, based on Shakespeare's *Tempest*, but instead he transmuted the material intended for the opera into an orchestral showpiece, which he called *Prospero's Spells*. This work was taken up enthusiastically by Bruno Walter, who insisted on substituting it for the scheduled item (Strauss's *Death and Transfiguration*) in a concert in Amsterdam in March 1938. Fateful decision. Wellesz was thus in Amsterdam attending rehearsals when he heard of the *Anschluss*. Friends advised him not to return to Vienna. A timely invitation arrived from London to collaborate on the fourth edition of Grove's *Dictionary of Music and Musicians*. He accepted and travelled to England. His family, temporarily left behind in Vienna, endured some hardships – his wife's passport was at first confiscated by the Gestapo – but were eventually able to follow him to England in July. His widow reported that he never considered leaving Austria before '38, even when he saw Schoenberg depart for the USA in 1933, or lived through the assassination of Austrian Chancellor Dollfuss in 1934.

Exiled in a new land, Wellesz was materially cushioned but artistically bereft. Sir Hugh Allen, one of his numerous English patrons, found him teaching work at Oxford. He was elected to a fellowship at Lincoln College in 1939, later becoming university lecturer and Reader in Byzantine Music. Like other "enemy aliens", he was interned for several months on the Isle of Man, until Vaughan Williams successfully interceded to secure his release. (Daniel Snowman reports in his book *The Hitler Emigrés* that Wellesz's lectures on Byzantine music provided one of the high-minded diversions with which the camp inmates filled their days). During the war he had various offers from American universities but decided to stay in Oxford, where he was part of a convivial exile community that included

Gerty von Hofmannsthal, widow of his old friend and collaborator. At first, the composer Wellesz fell silent. He continued his scholarship but composed nothing in England until 1943, when he began his Fifth String Quartet. This was followed, the next year, by a beautiful setting of Gerard Manley Hopkins's poem 'The Leaden Echo and the Golden Echo', which shows his sensitivity to the language of his new home. From then on, the music was unstoppable. Of his 112 numbered works, almost half were composed in England, where he remained for the rest of his life. Holidaying in the Lake District in summer 1945, he was reminded of the Salzkammergut – so much so that ideas for a symphony occurred to him, a form he had never written in before. Over the next 25 years he wrote nine symphonies – the canonical number, nine, of the Austro-German tradition – fine works which consciously reflect in their dimensions and orchestration the Vienna of Beethoven and Schubert, while synthesising in their language the Vienna of Wellesz's youth, of Mahler and Schoenberg. In later years he continued to combine composition with scholarship and teaching; his Oxford pupils now hold positions of authority in university music departments. Many are the anecdotes of hospitality enjoyed at 51 Woodstock Road, Oxford, what Wilfrid Mellers called the "sweet Viennese charm" of the Wellesz *ménage*. Perhaps Wellesz was aggrieved that, after the war, he was never invited back to Austria. He returned as a visitor, certainly – there were concerts of his music, state honours conferred on him – but no official position was offered to one of Austria's most eminent living musicians. He suffered a stroke in 1972, which prevented any further work, and died in 1974. He is buried in the Central Cemetery in Vienna, to which city his widow returned after his death and where she died in 1987.

[This was a rather dry talk I gave in London in June 2002 as part of the 'Continental Britons' festival at Wigmore Hall. For a magisterial treatment of a figure I've treated only summarily here, see Michael Haas's *Forbidden Music* (Yale UP, 2013) and his associated blog post on Wellesz. Also of importance is a recent book by Oxford musicologist Bojan Bujić, *Arnold Schoenberg and Egon Wellesz: A Fraught Relationship* (Plumbago, 2020).]

The Gender of Mr W. S.
(with apologies to Oscar Wilde)

I had been dining with Erskine in his pretty little house in Birdcage Walk, and we were sitting in the library over our coffee and cigarettes, when the question of Shakespeare's biography happened to turn up in conversation. I advanced the view that since Shakespeare died four hundred years ago, in the centuries since then, surely every wise thought that could be entertained about this author has been tested to destruction. Erskine, who was a good deal older than I was, listened to me with the amused deference of a man of forty, put his hand upon my shoulder and said: "Ah, but there is one idea that has never been taken seriously enough, although it bubbles under in the literature of the nineteenth and twentieth centuries... What if Shakespeare were what we would now term 'transgender'?"

The thought is not unthinkable. Indeed, as thought-experiments go, it's far less outlandish than some of the wilder biographical speculation that denies that a glover's son from Stratford could have written the plays attributed to him. We are still far from understanding the causes of gender variance, but the safest assumption is that, in its manifestations, we're looking at a combination of biological and environmental factors, of 'nature' and 'nurture'. If we further assume that its natural occurrence is roughly similar from generation to generation, even from century to century, then we would expect to encounter trans people four hundred years ago. But long before the concept existed, at a time when understanding of sex and gender was quite unlike our own, public perception would have been different; *self*-perception would have been different. Upbringing, education, legal sanctions: so many environmental constraints would have acted differently upon gender identities which we are now – belatedly – learning to recognise and accept.

Prove it! Well, of course, I can't. Any more than I can *prove* the Bard was a closet Catholic or a wife-deserter or a tax-dodger. As one editor of the Sonnets, Stephen Booth, has wryly observed: "William Shakespeare was almost certainly homosexual, bisexual or heterosexual. The sonnets provide no evidence on the matter." But that doesn't invalidate the thought-experiment, for I acknowledge from the outset that I'm not running my experiment on scientific principles. The assertion that 'Shakespeare was transgender' isn't 'falsifiable'. (Falsifiability is the belief that for any hypothesis to have credibility, it must be inherently disprovable before it can become accepted as a scientific hypothesis or theory.) But, if it *were* true, what consequences would follow?

If our Elizabethan were of artistic leanings, we might expect him to be drawn to a medium where a transgender sensibility could find expression. Centuries later, Virginia Woolf toured that realm in *Orlando*. But the novel, as a form, was barely in its infancy in the late sixteenth century. What had matured in leaps and bounds was the theatre. And the English theatre had a unique characteristic not shared by its Continental equivalents: the female parts were played by boys. It was a place where everyone was someone else – a stage, in every sense of the word, for the exploration of sex/gender difference.

Of all the theories advanced for what Shakespeare was up to in his 'lost years' this is the one I most like: that the stage-struck provincial joined Queen Elizabeth's Men in 1587, after the sudden death of actor William Knell in a fight while on a tour which passed through Stratford. The other actors shuffled up to cover the dead man's parts and young Will filled the vacancy – which brought him to London and theatreland. Once in the more tolerant ambience of the city, he consolidated his position as an actor, did a little play-doctoring and started writing, making himself by 1592 into what Robert Greene enviously called "an absolute *Johannes factotum...* in his owne conceit the onely Shake-scene in a country."

Over a twenty-year career, his plays would resort at intervals to 'travesty', often using a well-worn convention to hint at more subversive purposes. There are girls dressed as boys in *Two Gentlemen of Verona*, *The Merchant of Venice*, *As You Like It*, *Twelfth Night* and *Cymbeline*. There are expressions of "anxious masculinity" (to borrow Mark Breitenberg's phrase) in *The Merry Wives of Windsor*, *Antony and Cleopatra* and *The Taming of the Shrew* as male cross-dressing is either depicted or alluded to. Late in his career Shakespeare created a true hermaphrodite in Ariel (*The Tempest*). And in between he was writing those pesky sonnets, so apparently pregnant with meaning, so resistant to interpretation:

A woman's face with Nature's own hand painted
Hast thou, the master-mistress of my passion;
A woman's gentle heart, but not acquainted
With shifting change, as is false women's fashion;
An eye more bright than theirs, less false in rolling,
Gilding the object whereupon it gazeth;
A man in hue, all hues in his controlling,

Much steals men's eyes and women's souls amazeth.
And for a woman wert thou first created;
Till Nature, as she wrought thee, fell a-doting,
And by addition me of thee defeated,
By adding one thing to my purpose nothing.
But since she prick'd thee out for women's pleasure,
Mine be thy love and thy love's use their treasure. (Sonnet 20)

For anyone tempted down this speculative path, there would be much ground to cover. One must define terms. One must grapple with the peculiarities of Elizabethan and Jacobean attitudes to the 'sex-gender system'. There are the notorious pamphlets of the day excoriating the depravity of the theatre and the confused boundaries between male and female (*Hic mulier, Haec vir*). Then there are the plays themselves, not to mention those suggestive longer poems, *Venus and Adonis* and *The Rape of Lucrece*, which alone sufficed for Ted Hughes to derive an entire mythology in his frustrating study *Shakespeare and the Goddess of Complete Being*. Hughes eschewed Shakespeare criticism entirely; his book contains no bibliography and almost no references. The scholar cannot be so cavalier. But oh dear, how much reading one would have to do to become a Shakespeare 'expert'! And still, beyond all the specificities, lies the bigger question posed by Coleridge and Woolf: what is the relationship between androgyny and creativity?

In the absence of 'facts', it's always tempting to make them up. I was surprised to see, in a newspaper article by James Shapiro, an undoubted Shakespeare expert, how sympathetic he was to *Shakespeare in Love*, the movie. Enjoyable tosh, I thought. Still, fiction is next to 'faction' and faction is next to fact, so let's make it up, in this our non-scientific experiment. Let's suppose that we can reconstruct *Love's Labour's Won*, the notorious 'lost' play, and let's imagine this is the key to unlock the transgender Shakespeare. Perhaps the Bard went a little too far; that's why the play was suppressed and never printed...

But maybe I'm stumbling where I have no business – into the realm of wild biographical surmise. Perhaps all one can say with confidence is that in the richness and variegation of Shakespeare's writing, among so much else, there are figurations of what trans individuals feel. This is the line taken by Canadian professor Mary Ann Saunders, herself a trans woman, who finds resonance for her own experience in *The Tempest*. She likens the character of Ariel, an 'ayrie spirit' at the whim of Prospero's command, to transgender individuals who depend on medical practitioners to allow them to present in the embodiment they choose.[15]

At Yale, a petition was recently launched to 'decolonize' the English Department's course on 'Major English Poets'. The course requires the study of Chaucer, Spenser, Donne, Milton, Pope, Wordsworth, T.S. Eliot... and, yes, Shakespeare. One student, Adriana Miele, wrote a column in the *Yale Daily News* in which she criticised the course because while students "are taught how to analyse canonical literature works", they "are not taught to question why it is canonical, or the implications of canonical works that actively oppress and marginalise non-white, non-male, trans and queer people."

Some artists may canalise their creativity to *conceal* gender dissonance. Hemingway is often cited as the archetype of the macho prose stylist:

---

[15] Karen Wang, 'Exploring *The Tempest*'s Ariel as a lens to transgender individuals', *The Ubyssey*, 6 April 2016
http://ubyssey.ca/culture/exploring-the-tempest-ariel-as-a-lens-to-transgender-individuals-347/.

Ernest Hemingway would have died rather than get old. And he did. He shot himself. A short sentence. Anything rather than a long sentence, a life sentence. Death sentences are short and very, very manly. Life sentences aren't. They go on and on, all full of syntax and qualifying clauses and confusing references and getting old.[16]

This is handsomely put but obscures the evidence, especially from his unfinished novel *The Garden of Eden*, that the old bruiser was burdened with gender 'issues' a-plenty. In fact, it's not unusual for an artist to harness their transgender dreaming to the wagon of self-expression. Freud speculated when writing about Leonardo da Vinci that creative people possess greater cross-sex identification than others. In his *Table Talk* (September 1832) Coleridge said that a great mind has to be "androgynous". Virginia Woolf developed the idea in her classic essay of 1928, *A Room of One's Own*, where she asserted that to be an ideal writer, one ought to be

woman-manly or man-womanly… Some collaboration has to take place in the mind between the woman and the man before the art of creation can be accomplished. Some marriage of opposites has to be consummated.

She glossed Coleridge as meaning that the "androgynous mind" is a mind resistant to gender distinction: "He meant, perhaps, that the androgynous mind is resonant and porous; that it transmits emotion without impediment; that it is naturally creative, incandescent, and undivided." In her essay, Woolf praised a number of famous "androgynous" writers, including Shakespeare, Keats, Sterne, Cowper, Lamb, and Coleridge himself. She was unsure, however, of

---

[16] Ursula K. Le Guin, 'Introducing myself' in *The Wave in the Mind*, 2004.

the soundness of Milton and Jonson, Wordsworth and Tolstoy, saying that they had "a dash too much of the male", and Proust, since he was "a little too much of a woman."

Anyone brought up, like me, in the slipstream of the Women's Movement of the 1970s is schooled to be suspicious of such efforts to 'gender' the brain. But Woolf's argument, however time-bound its terminology, suggests something. And the anecdotal, if not the empirical evidence, is so strong that it's hard to resist.

I used to be friends with a talented classical musician. Her repertoire was dominated by Johannes Brahms. I once said to her, "You play a lot of Brahms, never Beethoven. Why is that?" Her reply came clearly from the heart, not from any feminist textbook: "Because Brahms is a *female* composer. Beethoven feels so *male*."

As I walked home through St. James's Park, reflecting upon Erskine's arguments, the dawn was just breaking over London. The white swans were lying asleep on the polished lake, and the gaunt Palace looked purple against the pale green sky. It occurred to me that we have no right to quarrel with an artist for the conditions under which he chooses to present his work, all Art being to a certain degree a mode of acting, an attempt to realise one's own personality on some imaginative plane out of reach of the trammelling accidents and limitations of real life. We are such stuff as dreams are made on.

The Electric Body: Nancy Cunard Sees Josephine Baker

On 22 September 1925 the Cunard liner *Berengaria* docked at Cherbourg. Among the disembarking passengers was a group of African Americans. They were the cast of a revue, hastily assembled in New York by a white American socialite and would-be impresario, Caroline Dudley Reagan, and booked into the Théâtre des Champs Élysées, Paris. The show, which they had begun to rehearse only on the transatlantic crossing, was called *La Revue Nègre*. It was Dudley's attempt to show Parisians 'real' Negro music and dance and to capitalise on the French cultural elite's obsession with what became known in the 1920s as *'négrophilie'*. By the time the show opened on 2 October it had been transformed from a vaudeville conceived for a white American public into a more complex music-hall production adapted to French tastes. It is instructive to follow through the reaction of one audience member – the writer, publisher, civil rights activist and society rebel Nancy Cunard – to see how black dance was read by one of its more thoughtful white afficianados.

The show began with a big ensemble number – a Mississippi river dock scene – introducing all twenty-five performers. As the scene climaxed, there was an extraordinary apparition, described thus by French critic Pierre de Régnier:

A strange figure in a ragged undershirt ambles onto the stage looking like a cross between a boxing kangaroo and a racing driver... She is in constant motion, her body writhing like a snake or more precisely like a dipping saxophone. Music seems to pour from her body. She grimaces, crosses her eyes, wiggles disjointedly, does a split and finally crawls off the stage stiff-legged, her rump higher than her head, like a young giraffe.

They had to wait for the finale to see more of her. With partner Joe Alex she executed a sort of improvised *pas de deux*, billed as a "danse sauvage". Many years later Janet Flanner, the veteran *New Yorker* correspondent, recalled the impact of that "savage dance":

She made her entry entirely nude except for a pink flamingo feather between her limbs; she was being carried upside down and doing the split on the shoulder of a black giant. Midstage he paused, and with his long fingers holding her basket-wise around the waist, swung her in a slow cartwheel to the stage floor, where she stood, like his magnificent discarded burden, in an instant of complete silence... A scream of salutation spread through the theatre. Whatever happened next was unimportant. The two specific elements had been established and were unforgettable – her magnificent dark body, a new model that to the French proved for the first time that black was beautiful, and the acute response of the white masculine public in the capital of hedonism of all Europe – Paris.

This was a new star, Josephine Baker. Flanner was absolutely right about the "white masculine public". A brief survey of the Paris-based critics of the day shows that, however they dressed it up in aesthetic garb, however worthily their reviews invoked the names of Rousseau and Bougainville, their "acute responses" were markedly sexualised. In modern parlance, Baker was "pure theatrical Viagra". Critics routinely emphasised her "animality" and "primitiveness". To e.e. cummings she was "a creature neither infrahuman nor superhuman but somehow both: a mysteriously unkillable Something". To dance critic André Levinson the "undeniable rhythmic superiority of these negro dancers is nothing less than an adjunct of their irrepressible animality". To another critic she is "this gracious little exotic animal… who teaches us about the brutality only certain races have". Le Corbusier devised a ballet scenario for her in which he imagined her "dressed as a monkey". Critics had two ways of investing importance in Baker and rescuing her from their own fantasies of the exotic. One was to identify her as living sculpture. Thus Levinson read her as a "black Venus" in whom "the plastic sense of a race of sculptors and the frenzy of the African Eros swept over the audience". The other was to represent her as an "ambassador from the jungle" come to redeem an effete European civilisation. Paul Brach thanked her for "abandoning the heat of a tropical river" to "breathe on the banks of the Seine and unto our grey and tired lives". The critic of *Volonté* believed she held the secret that would spare the great cities of the world from "dying from the weight of civilisation". The artist Paul Colin, whose images of Baker and posters for *La Revue Nègre* did so much to establish her iconography, speculated that her dances foretold the "era of a new civilisation, finally relieved of fetters centuries old". Of course, these were canny men who knew perfectly well that Baker had never been any place near a tropical river. Robert de Flers in *Le Figaro* countered that, far from redeeming civilisation, poor and uneducated black performers like Baker were the "dregs" of modern civilisation. Arnold Haskell, the English dance critic, wrote that she "always seemed to be playing up to what the public wants the negro to be". Black artist and Parisian 'negrophile' were locked into a nexus of supply and demand.

If it is true that Baker was only ever 'performing' primitivism, can we still find significance in her dancing? Baker's improvisations transgressed the conventions of choreographed dance; she strung together steps with every appearance of spontaneity. Where European dancers showed the front, presenting the body as a unified line, Baker contrived to move different parts of her body to different rhythms. Most shocking to dance purists, she used her backside, shaking it, as one of her biographers says, as though it were an instrument. The embodiedness of this dance was new, at least outside folk traditions. Where European classical dancers strive upward, she was grounded. According to Levinson, where in the European tradition the harmony between the movement of the body and the rhythm of the music is constant and tacit, Baker's dancing was based upon direct and audible expression of the rhythm. "Negroes dance with their senses," wrote Ivan Goll, "while Europeans can only dance with their minds". Such black dance challenged two trends in European dance which, arguably, by the 1920s were losing vitality: the high art tradition of the Ballets Russes and the 'expressive dance' movement of performers like Mary Wigman and Isadora Duncan. Ironically, both trends had associations with the Théâtre des Champs-Élysées (where the *Revue Nègre* revue show premiered). Before it changed ownership the theatre had been home to Diaghilev's company when in Paris; it was the scene of the scandalous premiere of *The Rite of Spring* in 1913. A piece in *Vogue*, February 1925, ventures the opinion that "the Negro... dances better than Nijinsky". Blaise Cendrars compared Jean Börlin's dancing in *La Création du Monde* to that of a "mulatto, Negro... With your

Swedish peasant feet, you are the exact opposite of the Ballets Russes". The interior of the Théâtre des Champs-Élysées is decorated with frescoes by Maurice Denis depicting Isadora Duncan barefoot, in flowing tunics. Baker's style was compared by some critics to the freedom of movement that Isadora Duncan championed for dancing. The Greek-inspired Duncan was horrified, and wrote: "It seems to me monstrous that anyone should believe that the jazz rhythm expresses America". Duncan's art, like the 'serpentine dances' of her predecessor Loie Fuller, depended on the skilful extension of the body through costume. In a joky reference to the fairytale of the Emperor's New Clothes, Baker once implied that, since she wore (almost) no clothes in her act, *she* had created an art of pure essence.

Somewhere among the testosterone-rich early audiences of *La Revue Nègre* was Nancy Cunard, in Parisian self-exile. Before turning to Cunard's reception of Baker, it is worth attempting a comparison between these two women. Baker was born in 1906 in the slums of East St Louis, the illegitimate daughter of a washed-up song-and-dance pair. Her father left within a year of Josephine's birth. Her mother took up with another man and bore him three children. Her natural father had Hispanic blood; her stepfather was much darker-skinned, and so were her step-siblings. She claimed that her mother rejected her for "not being black enough"; auditioning later for Broadway shows, she was rejected for being "too black". From her neighbours she learned the latest steps and dances – the 'Mess Around', the 'Itch' – as they passed through black urban centres. Driven by the need to escape the poverty of this upbringing, she hung around theatres, working her way up from dresser to comic chorus girl. By March 1924 she finally reached New York in the chorus of an all-black show, *Chocolate Dandies*. Even then, specialised as a comedienne and novelty dancer, she gave little forewarning of her subsequent transformations. But she announced it as soon as she reached Paris. Paul Colin, unhappy with her 'made in Harlem' outfits, marched her off to the couturier Poiret. As Baker herself puts it in one of several rewritings of her life story: "Since I personified the savage on the stage, I tried to be as civilised as possible in daily life". The same journalists who had watched her 'animal' performance in *La Revue Nègre* covered her arrival at the first night party, now fully and fashionably clothed: "At heart, perhaps, this pretty little 'savage' is well and truly Parisian," wrote Henri Jeanson. A cartoon of 1926 depicts her as a society lady with a monkey's tail protruding from her dress. This is the key to her self-creation over the next ten years. Initially, her performances were full of leaping and acrobatics, of a sort that her audience read as 'animal'. But as she in turn read her audience, her imagery became more sophisticated. The animality was externalised. Many iconic images show her, elegantly dressed, with her pet leopard Chiquita. She took French lessons. Gradually, the singing took over from the dancing. Janet Flanner's column from 1930 shows how equivocally this development was viewed by her earliest admirers:

Miss Baker... has, alas, almost become a little lady. Her caramel-coloured body, which overnight became a legend in Europe, is still magnificent, but it has become thinned, trained, almost civilised... There is a rumour that she wants to sing refined ballads; one is surprised that she doesn't want to play Othello. On that lovely animal visage lies now a sad look, not of captivity, but of dawning intelligence.

But it was too late for such regrets. Baker had discovered that she could play the *chanteuse*, as successfully as she had played the "pretty little savage". She even made a bid for literary status. She opened her own night-club, Chez Josephine, with a house magazine featuring art work, fashion and poems. In 1930 a novel appeared under her name. *Mon sang dans tes veines* (My blood in your veins) is a parable about interracial love. The black heroine dies in the act of giving a blood transfusion to her estranged white boyfriend, the mixed blood in his veins now meaning that he can never marry the pretty (white) flapper to whom he has since become engaged. How much of this farrago is Baker's work, how much that of her two credited collaborators, is unknown. All this activity brought Baker immense fame and a considerable income. Her marriage in 1927 to a self-styled Italian 'Count' confirmed her conquest of, and assimilation into, white Paris.

The contrast with her admirer Nancy Cunard could hardly be greater. Born into a life of ease, her literary success speeded along by her mother's social contacts with editors, Cunard too broke with her ancestry, identifying with the racial 'other'. The famous photographs of her – by Man Ray and Cecil Beaton – are exercises in self-construction, as surely as when Baker poses with the pet leopard or, her face whitened by the heaviest makeup, is photographed on the arm of 'Count' Abatino. Baker, by the 1930s, was very rich; Cunard, after the breach with her mother, Lady Emerald, was most probably not. Jane Marcus has written fascinatingly about photographs of Cunard taken by Barbara Ker-Seymer employing the 'solarization' technique – negative prints which made the white subject appear black. Is it fanciful to read 'Josephine Baker' as a 'solarization' of 'Nancy Cunard', the skin tones reversed, the career paths running in opposite directions? And, if so, can this be a subtext in Cunard's troubled reading of Baker?

In a revealing autobiographical passage Cunard recalls her childhood dreams about black Africa,

with Africans dancing and drumming around me, and I one of them, though still white, knowing, mysteriously enough, how to dance in their own manner. Everything was full of movement in these dreams; it was that which enabled me to escape in the end, going further, even further!

Here is a self-identification with black dance as a means of escape and self-abandon from what 'civilisation' had made her. Raymond Mortimer said that what first struck him about Cunard was her *"regard"* – he uses the French word to mean not only the eyes "but the way in which they confront the visible world". Sight is no less subjective than the other senses. What those "Arctic blue" eyes of Mortimer's description 'saw' when they 'saw' Baker was what they wanted to see: a promise of escape, an image of female self-abandon, or a betrayal of both those things.

To my knowledge, Cunard only wrote about Baker on two occasions. The first was in a despatch from Paris for *Vogue* in May 1926. Here she writes about the new show at the Folies Bergère. *La Folie du Jour*, Baker's first Paris show as headliner, was designed to exploit the contrast of 'culture' and 'nature'. The lengthy warm-up before the star's entrance had eight scantily clad girls being shown the wealth of Paris. As each girl selected fashionable clothes from among those on show, she left the stage more fully dressed than she entered. Then Baker made her entrance, reversing this recapitulation of cultural 'evolution'. Baker was the 'savage' Fatou, wearing only her famous girdle of bananas. As she danced, the bananas bounced and bobbed like so many flaccid (but perhaps, in the imagination of her audience, tumescent) phalluses. In her review for *Vogue*, Cunard unashamedly sides with 'nature' against 'culture'. She deprecates the "interminable series of naked women contraptioned into fans" but revels in "the perfect delight one gets from Josephine Baker, most astounding of mulatto dancers, in her necklets, bracelets, and flouncing feathered loincloths" as she "contorts her surprising form through a maze of complicated rhythms". Baker is even better on her own here, Cunard believes, than when surrounded by the troupe of the *Revue Nègre* the previous autumn. Little is made here of Baker's blackness – instead, Cunard defines the dancer's 'otherness' in terms of outlandish appearance and physical versatility – nor of her nakedness, which Cunard evidently reads as 'natural', unlike the confected eroticism of the white chorus-line.

Cunard's *regard* was turned on Baker a second time in one of her own contributions to the *Negro* anthology, the vast anthology of African-American literature and art which she edited and which, apart from her colourful life, remains her greatest achievement. By the 1930s, as we have seen, Baker's public image had had a consummate make-over. This was confirmed by her show *La Joie de Paris*, which opened at the Casino de Paris in December 1932. Baker had been taking ballet lessons with Balanchine and in the new show, distancing herself from the barefoot 'Fatou' of her early years, performed in ballet shoes for the first time. Having worked on her voice as well, she sang a lot more. One of her numbers was a skit on the growing fad for sunbathing, 'Si j'étais blanche', with a lyric suggesting that Baker was now lighter skinned than a lot of tanned Parisiennes. For this she wore a platinum wig of marcelled ringlets. This song had a serious undertow, for, from her earliest appearances at the Folies Bergère, Baker had rubbed her skin with lemon juice in an attempt to make it seem lighter. All this was too much for her erstwhile fan Nancy Cunard. In the piece for *Negro*, Cunard quotes several "dreary" French critics who exult at Baker's transformation:

Civilisation has done its work – Josephine is from now on assimilated by the western world… she seems to whiten as we gaze at her – by far the best example of the perfecting of the black race by its intellectual contact with European civilisation.

This was a travesty of what Cunard had first seen in the *Revue Nègre*: "the magnificent tornado, the wild-fire syncopation of Josephine Baker's beautiful brown electric body". Her dancing "could be compared to the purest of African plastic in motion – it was *free*, perfect and exact, it centred admirably in the spare gold banana fronds round the dynamic hips". The tyranny of French "national taste" is read by Cunard as a form of "nationalism and colonisation" (her phrase) every bit as insidious as that in English-speaking countries. Baker, says Cunard, is "so supreme of her type as to be – paradoxically sounding – *unique*". In seeking to make of Baker a "whitened, gallicised actress," French critics have mistyped her. But what 'type' is she supposed to be? According to her biographer, Cunard often expressed the wish that her black American lover Henry Crowder had a darker skin or behaved in a more primitive, exotic manner. "Be more *African*," she reportedly told him. She had similar aspirations for Baker (although, so far as we know, they never met). The Baker whom she had first seen in 1925, the 'savage' dancer, this was the 'authentic' Baker, whose subsequent transformations were a betrayal imposed on her by her new host country.

Cunard saw what she saw. Looking back nearly a century later, we may see differently. For me there are two problems with Cunard's reading, and they are linked. One is a racial essentialism that expects the African-American performer to embody the 'primitive'. The other is a denial of Baker's own agency. Cunard implies that Baker has been made over by the French critics – and made over into something that she was not, a betrayal of her 'type'. In fact, Baker was a chameleon who profited from a benign conspiracy with her Paris public. Each side willed the same outcome, but for different reasons. Paris could interpret her success as a triumph of France's civilising mission; she could see it as outperforming the whites at their own game, most visibly by toppling Mistinguett, the previous (white) queen of Paris revue. Baker's willingness to be what the public wanted – by turns, 'savage' dancer, sophisticated cabaret artiste – can be read many ways, as a psychological need rooted in her childhood, as the socioeconomic imperative of the poor black who had traditionally developed mimicry as a survival technique in white society. However, I think these metamorphoses were willingly undergone, not least because it was a gratification to discover in herself the technical abilities to carry them off. The young Cunard, "though still white", had known, "mysteriously enough", how to do the 'savage dance'. In Baker she found her solarized self, a black woman who did the 'savage dance' for a living. But when Baker asserted her independence from stereotypes of blackness and hung up her bananas, Cunard could not follow her. Their paths did not cross again.

Sources

Petrine Archer-Straw, *Negrophilia: Avant-Garde Paris and Black Culture in the 1920s* (2000)

Anne Anlin Cheng, *Second Skin: Josephine Baker and the Modern Surface* (2010)

Anne Chisholm, *Nancy Cunard* (1979)

Janet Flanner, *Paris Was Yesterday 1925-1939* (1973)

Sieglinde Lemke, *Primitivist Modernism: Black Culture and the Origins of Transatlantic Modernism* (1998)

Jane Marcus, 'Bonding and Bondage: Nancy Cunard and the Making of the *Negro* Anthology', in *Borders, Boundaries and Frames: Essays in Cultural Criticism and Cultural Studies*, ed. Mae G. Henderson (1995)

Ean Wood, *The Josephine Baker Story* (2000)

Hedy Lamarr

In Vienna in the first half of the twentieth century, so many people of note sprang from the culture of assimilated Jewry that was among the city's distinct glories. One of them was Hedy Lamarr.

Born Hedwig Kiesler in the Austrian capital in 1914, she was stage-struck from childhood. A brief early film career was notable for the Czech film *Ecstasy* (1933). This controversial appearance would haunt her for the rest of her life, thanks to Hedy's brief nude scenes and what was supposedly the first representation of female orgasm on screen. As the resulting hullabaloo continued, she found a role on stage in *Sissy*, a musical comedy by Fritz Kreisler about the courtship of the future Empress of Austria by the young Franz Josef. During the theatrical run, the most persistent of her stage-door Johnnies was one Fritz Mandl, an arms manufacturer and the third richest man in Austria. His persistence paid off; her acquiescence to flattery did not. She soon found herself married to a controlling bigot who snuffed out her acting ambitions and treated her as little more than arm-candy. Escaping to Paris and thence to London, she engineered a meeting with MGM studio head Louis B. Mayer, who'd crossed the Atlantic to scout for European talent. He offered her a movie contract in Hollywood. It was on their voyage back to the States in 1937 that Mayer and his wife came up with the Austrian's new moniker, adapting the name of silent-film actress Barbara La Marr, who'd died some years earlier of tuberculosis. "We are going to replace death with life," Mayer declared.

Image would be everything. The studio photos of Hedy are indeed stunning. The raven-black hair with distinctive centre parting convinced the public that 'bombshells' didn't have to be blonde. But she was also a blank canvas onto which the audience could project. One of her most devoted fans was the American artist Joseph Cornell. During the war Cornell tried to befriend the star by sending her admiring letters, which she graciously replied to. He channelled his enthusiasm into a remarkable collage, titled 'Enchanted Wanderer'. By inserting a publicity photo of Hedy's face into a reproduction of a Giorgione portrait of a Renaissance boy, he subverted the gendered 'sex appeal' that Holly-wood worked so hard to create through photography. "She has slipped effortlessly into the role of a painter herself," Cornell suggested in an effusive text accompanying his image, one "who again speaks the poetic and evocative language of the silent film, if only in whispers at times, beside the empty roar of the soundtrack."

I wish I could enthuse like Cornell about Hedy's Holly-wood movies. She's a lustrous screen presence, for sure; not a *great* actress, but possessed of a deft touch in light romantic comedy. In more challenging roles – *The Strange Woman* (1946), for example, where she plays a scheming beauty who is both ministering angel and accessory to murder – her limitations are tested. But I wouldn't go as far as Parker Tyler who, in his 1944 study *The Hollywood Hallucination*, numbered Hedy among cinema's "som-nambules", those "ladies with sleep in their eyes" who radiated an "unquestionable impression of nocturnal acquiescence". For Tyler, the *showgirl* was the purest somnambulistic type of all, an "animated odalisque" who neither speaks nor is spoken to. Packaged as an exotic mannequin, Hedy played such a showgirl in *Ziegfeld Girl* (1941), but her talents are sorely underused.

There were missed opportunities to raise her game. In 1942 Mayer refused to loan her out to Warner Brothers, so she never got to play opposite Humphrey Bogart in *Casablanca*. She turned down offers to star in two *film noir* classics – *Laura* and *Gaslight* – ceding the ground to Gene Tierney and Ingrid Bergman, respectively.

Nowadays, people are as interested in her life off-screen as on it. Take, for example, the fact that she was inducted into the National Inventors Hall of Fame in 2014: how does that relate to her film roles?

In *Dishonored Lady* (1947) she plays a career woman who attempts suicide. Quitting her job as art editor on an upmarket magazine, she changes her name and lifestyle and puts her ambitions on hold. She takes up painting – although this activity seems to be more therapeutic than professional – and becomes the dutiful helpmate to a successful research scientist, whom she finally marries. The conservative message is clear: women belong in the kitchen, not the lab; the bedroom, not the boardroom. As a male admirer tells her early in the film, "You don't look like an art editor, more like a work of art!"

In *Let's Live A Little* (1948), Robert Cummings plays a woman-hating ad man who is despatched to a psychiatrist to cure his misogyny. Cue much mirth when Cummings discovers that this mind-doctor is a *lady* doctor, the luscious Hedy Lamarr no less. Romance develops as Hedy falls for her patient and he struggles to overcome his native aversion to the female of the species. It's another veiled warning about the perils awaiting the professional woman. Women are emotional creatures, and emotion will out.

What's striking is how these frivolous plotlines follow some of the contours of Hedy's own life: a fact of which the original filmmakers were surely unaware. Tagged forever as "the most beautiful woman in the world", she was never going to be taken seriously in any serious pursuit. Yet scientific invention had been a hobby since her girlhood. Her father, to whom she was devoted, had encouraged her to take an interest in technology. There are suggestions that, as she prettily hosted Mandl's dinner parties for the Viennese elite in the 1930s, she was quietly attending to the men's discussion of weapons development. At the beginning of World War II, she and composer George Antheil developed a radio guidance system for Allied torpedoes that used spread spectrum and frequency hopping technology to defeat the threat of jamming by the Axis powers. Although the US Navy didn't adopt the technology until the 1960s, the principles of their work are incorporated into the Bluetooth and GPS technology used today. Hence the belated laurels from the National Inventors.

Hedy made her last movie in 1957: in *The Female Animal* she portrayed a glamorous but faded actress who takes up with a toy-boy. As her biographer Ruth Barton observes, the production team clearly had *Sunset Boulevard* in mind, but neither director nor cast was able to re-create Billy Wilder's masterpiece. In later years, Hedy seemed like so many of Hollywood's *grandes dames* to retreat into Norma Desmond-style seclusion. There was botched plastic surgery. There was pointless litigation: against Mel Brooks when he wrote a villain called 'Hedley Lamarr' into his spoof western *Blazing Saddles*; and against the publisher of her own autobiography, *Ecstasy and Me*, borne of the belief that she'd been traduced by her ghost writer. She died in 2000, having notched up a further five marriages since her divorce from

Mandl. In accordance with her last wishes, her son Anthony Loder spread her ashes in the Vienna Woods: a return to the soil from which she'd sprung.

Louise Brooks

On 2 May 1978 Kenneth Tynan rang the doorbell of a modest two-room apartment in Rochester, New York. The person he'd come to meet had obsessed him for decades; once he'd even 'dragged up' as her to attend a fancy-dress ball. Until a few months earlier he had assumed she was dead:

After a long pause, there was a loud snapping of locks. The door slowly opened to reveal a petite woman of fragile build, wearing a woollen bed jacket over a pink nightgown, and holding herself defiantly upright by means of a sturdy metal cane with four rubber-tipped prongs. She had salt-and-pepper hair combed back into a ponytail that hung down well below her shoulders, and she was barefoot.

"You're doing a terrible thing to me," she told her visitor as she let him in. "I've been killing myself off for twenty years, and you're going to bring me back to life."

This was the legendary Louise Brooks, and Tynan – dramaturge, impresario, titan of drama critics – was to profile her for the *New Yorker*. Over the course of three days, they talked. The 71-year-old Brooks was plagued by arthritis, so she reclined on her bed while Tynan pulled up a chair beside her. Out from her wardrobe tumbled a lifetime of photographs and mementos, prompting a flood of reminiscence, which, together with the many letters she wrote him after their meeting, Tynan worked up into a near 20,000-word article. Each was in awe of the other: Brooks admired Tynan's critical writing, the finest she thought since Bernard Shaw; as for Tynan, his interviewee was "the only star actress I can imagine either being enslaved by or wanting to enslave; and a dark lady worthy of any poet's devotion."

Tynan was a difficult man. His rackety private life, his interest in the wilder shores of sexual experimentation (expressed in the pet project of his later life, the revue *Oh! Calcutta!*), threaten to overshadow his reputation as a writer. But I'm with the late Clive James who once offered this advice to the aspiring critic:

Any youngster who wants to get into this business should find a copy of Tynan's first book, *He That Plays the King*, and do what I did – sit down and read it aloud paragraph by paragraph. It will soon be seen that his sometimes pedestrian radical opinions were far outstripped by his perceptions, which moved like lightning to energize almost every sentence.[17]

The story of Tynan's encounter with the "ravishing hermit of Rochester", as he called her, is deftly told in a chapter of Kathleen Tynan's biography of her husband. I recommend it. For me, reading Kathleen's account alongside Tynan's original *New Yorker* essay had the function of all good criticism – it sent me back to the subject...

---

[17] Clive James, *North Face of Soho: Unreliable Memoirs Volume IV*. Tynan himself had a surprising apprentice-master in his Oxford tutor, C.S. Lewis. Under the Oxford system, an undergraduate would normally read out his essays to his tutor. In his *Diaries* (entry for 1 October 1974), Tynan recalls that "because I stammered, [Lewis] kindly undertook to read my weekly essays aloud for me, and the prospect of hearing my words pronounced in that wonderfully juicy and judicious voice had a permanently disciplining effect on my prose style."

Ah, Louise Brooks… How do I love thee? Let me count the ways. That luminous face "framed in its black proscenium arch of hair" (as Tynan puts it)… What a *Photoplay* journalist in 1926 called her "lyric legs"… But an actor's body is only equipment, surely? Did not Brooks herself write that "the great art of films does not consist in descriptive movement of face and body, but in the movements of thought and soul transmitted in a kind of intense isolation"?

Let's consider her more soberly.

Born in Kansas in 1906, she began her career as a dancer, training under that pioneer of modern dance, Ruth St Denis. By way of a stint in the Ziegfeld Follies, she won her way to a screen test with Paramount. Her film career was short; she appeared in 24 films between 1925 and 1938. Several of those from the silent era are lost or survive only as fragments, and in few of her films is she the lead. I can't claim much acquaintance with her Hollywood work – Tynan dismisses most of them as "assembly-line studio products" – but I know that one of the better ones, *A Girl in Every Port* (1928), was seen by G. W. Pabst, the great Austrian director, who spotted a potential in her that had eluded American eyes. Transported to Berlin after Pabst had despaired of finding a European actress to play Wedekind's Lulu, she made under his tutelage two of the greatest films of the silent era: *Pandora's Box* (1929) and *Diary of a Lost Girl* (1929). They both have the power to shock, even today, but achieve their effects with a rare combination of forthrightness yoked to subtlety.

Tynan observed that *Pandora's Box* "could easily have emerged as a cautionary tale about a *grande cocotte* whose reward is the wages of sin." Instead, he identified "moral coolness" as the predominant tone:

[The film] assumes neither the existence of sin nor the necessity for retribution. It presents a series of events in which all the participants are seeking happiness, and it suggests that Lulu, whose notion of happiness is momentary fulfilment through sex, is not less admirable than those whose quest is for wealth or social advancement.

In the course of conversation, Tynan suggested to Brooks that "the film takes the play and turns it upside down. It doesn't make [Lulu] a destroyer of men." In this opinion he was in line with another of the actress's legion of admirers – Angela Carter. In the late 1980s Carter was approached by Richard Eyre, director of the UK's National Theatre, to write a modern version of Wedekind's 'Lulu' plays. Initially enthusiastic, she cooled towards the project when she read the originals. While Pabst and Brooks had sought to discredit the myth of the *femme fatale*, she felt that Wedekind had remained in its thrall, serving up a character "who must die because she is free". (In Wedekind's defence, one might argue that his character is richly ambiguous. Yes, she lacks agency, inspiring evil unaware, but acts as a reflector or refractor of male perceptions of women.)

Two characteristics of Brooks's performance forever beguile me. One is how, true to her training, she always moves – and sits, and stands – like a dancer. There is a scene in *Pandora's Box* where Schigolch, Lulu's elderly 'patron', is rehearsing her in a dance number. It was only after filming this scene that Pabst realised that the actress he had cast on sight was a professional dancer. "It was the moment when he realised all his intuitions about me were right," Brooks reflected later. In this sense, she was the ideal star for the silent screen, where gesture, movement, bodily inflection must do much of the work of dialogue. However, her other characteristic takes us above and beyond the limitations of that era before 'talkies' and propels her into the present day. I refer to the restrained naturalism of her acting style. When the Lulu film first appeared, German critics were baffled: "Louise Brooks cannot act. She does not suffer. She does nothing" was a typical complaint. For those accustomed to the exaggerated posturing of many actors of the period, whose technique derived from the theatre, this was new. "Less is more" should be the screen actor's watchword: a close-up can record a flutter of the eyelids that would be imperceptible to an audience far from the stage in conventional theatre. Pabst knew this, and Louise Brooks knew it too.

Tynan suggested that 'The Education of Lulu' would make an apt alternative title for *Diary of a Lost Girl*, "whose heroine emerges from her travails ideally equipped for the leading role in *Pandora's Box*." He is right that this film, although made later, functions a little like a 'prequel' – and would have looked even more like one if Pabst's original, tougher conception had survived censorship. Here, the theme, derived from a novel by Margarete Böhme, is the corruption of a minor and the hypocrisy of the authoritarian society that surrounds her. Brooks plays Thymian Henning, a trusting young girl who is seduced and impregnated by an employee of her father, forced to give up her baby and then incarcerated in a brutal reform school for delinquents, from which she escapes. Following a series of adventures – including employment in an upmarket brothel – she makes an advantageous marriage and ends up, ironically, as a trustee of the very reformatory where she had once been imprisoned. Brooks's biographer Barry Paris argues that the actress was never more erotic than in the bordello scenes, "dancing, drinking champagne, arching her swanlike neck in full sexual submission", and it's hard to disagree.

Brooks returned to Hollywood in the Thirties but found herself reduced to accepting parts in B-movies. Disgusted by a studio system that seemed unable to accommodate her, she moved to New York. "Your life is exactly like Lulu's," Pabst had warned her, "and you will end the same way". Sure enough, she fell into financial hardship and at one point even became a paid escort. For the next two decades, she struggled with alcoholism and suicidal tendencies. But, happily, her work was rediscovered by cineastes in the 1950s, leading to a kind of resurrection. Late in life she discovered a talent for writing and produced a series of brilliant essays on the film industry and the many figures within it she had known (collected as *Lulu in Hollywood*, 1982). She died in 1985 in Rochester, N.Y., where she had moved to be close to the film archive of the George Eastman House.

One of those late articles was called 'Why I Will Never Write My Memoirs'. She characterised herself as a typical Midwesterner, "born in the Bible Belt of Anglo-Saxon farmers, who prayed in the parlour and practised incest in the barn." This was her conclusion:

In writing the history of a life I believe absolutely that the reader cannot understand the character and deeds of the subject unless he is given a basic understanding of that person's sexual loves and hates and conflicts. It is the only way the reader can make sense out of innumerable apparently senseless actions... We flatter ourselves when we assume that we have restored the sexual integrity which was expurgated by the Victorians. It is true that many exposés are written to shock, to excite, to make money. But in serious books characters remain as baffling, as unknowable as ever... I too am unwilling to write the sexual truth that would make my life worth reading. I cannot unbuckle the Bible Belt.

Both Brooks and Tynan were sexual adventurers. When

Tynan submitted his profile of the actress to the *New Yorker*, it was with a covering note apologising for one or two passages that were "more explicit than the magazine may care for. In their defence, I can only say that Miss B made her name in erotic roles and that she talks about sex as openly as you or I might talk about the weather." Brooks might never have written her memoirs (there was a false start in the 1940s which she consigned to the incinerator) but in Kenneth Tynan she found an ideal confidant and expositor.

Wedekind in English

From *Mine-Haha* to the plays

At the heart of a forest lies a mysterious girls' boarding school, cut off from the outside world by a great wall and barred gates. Within, a group of youngsters gather round a small coffin, from which emerges a new pupil, Hidalla...

Frank Wedekind (1864-1918) has always fascinated me. He seems like a man born out of his time. You look at photos of him taken over a hundred years ago singing self-composed songs to his own accompaniment and you think of a troubadour like Bob Dylan in his grizzled later incarnations. So it was fitting that I was led to *Mine-Haha* by one of the *grandes dames* of rock'n'roll, Marianne Faithfull. In her latest volume of memoirs she writes about Wedekind's strange novella, speculating on similarities to her own upbringing among the Braziers Park community and regretting that it had never been translated into English. Here was my cue. I had already translated *Franziska*, one of Wedekind's lesser-known plays, for a production at London's Gate Theatre, so I was no stranger to his bizarre world. What encouraged me is how others feel at home there too. As I worked on the text from around 2008, I discovered *Innocence*, the beautiful French film version of *Mine-Haha*. Then the Broadway rock musical *Spring Awakening* opened in London. In summer 2009 *Lulu*, Berg's opera based on two Wedekind plays, was revived at Covent Garden. And in 2010 Wedekind hit the London stage yet again, with emergent director Anna Ledwich bringing her adaptation of the 'Lulu' plays to the Gate Theatre in June.

In *Mine-Haha*, his most substantial prose text, Wedekind rehearses the concerns of his dramas – childhood, education, sexual awakening, the status of women – in concentrated fairytale form. It felt as if its time had come.

Rupert Brooke, I learnt with interest, was a Wedekind enthusiast. He admired the mixture of tragedy and farce, the way his characters' actions and speeches have "the inconsequence and abruptness of life" in contrast to those "rationalist playwrights, whose characters not only know but *say* what they're going to do before they do it." Holed up in Berlin in April 1912, Brooke went to see *Frühlings Erwachen* (Spring Awakening). He reported back to James Strachey:

I fairly held my breath when the curtains went up on darkness & the lady kept screaming "You're near enough, Melchior!" & at length there was a pop, & he was all too near, in fact, right inside. But when the lights returned the Fräulein all round, bless 'em, hadn't turned a hair. I was the only pink thing in the whole blessed Kreisenerspiele.

Thereafter for several months he was blowing hot and cold about translating this and other Wedekind plays into English. In August, back in London, he was in discussion with the publisher Stephen Swift about securing copyright. 'Stephen Swift' was actually a pseudonym of one Charles Hosken, a gentleman trickster who might have stepped out of the pages of a Patrick Hamilton novel. Brooke believed the publisher's real name to be 'Charles Granville', but this was in fact another of his aliases. As the original backer of *Rhythm* (the short-lived literary magazine edited by John Middleton Murry and Katherine Mansfield) and the publisher of *In a German Pension* (Mansfield's first short-story collection), Hosken/Granville/Swift deserves a footnote in literary history. However, in October 1912 he was wanted for embezzlement and bigamy, and fled the country. He was brought back, tried, and imprisoned for both offences, and his publishing company liquidated. This may explain why Brooke's translation of *Spring Awakening* proceeded no further than the opening scene (preserved among the Brooke papers in King's College, Cambridge). The poet was stumped by some of Wedekind's vocabulary – a loose-leaf sheet appended to the manuscript reads "How near any dialect is it? Or lower-class colloquialism?" – but it's a heroic stab at a difficult text and I rather wish he'd finished the job.

Spring Awakening: A New Musical (London, 2009)

I seemed to be in a minority of one, but I didn't 'get' this show. More of a Sondheim man, me. I had the sense that the authors had taken two historically determined phenomena and yoked them by violence together. On one hand there's Wedekind's original play, a daring presentation of coming-of-age in late nineteenth century Germany, where adults conspire to keep adolescents in ignorance of their own sexual awakening. On the other we're treated to a rock concert, using a musical language which has developed since the late 1950s alongside the invention of the 'teenager' and the unfolding of the 'permissive society', a language which expresses the knowingness of our sex-saturated culture.

Duncan Sheik (composer) has said that what he dislikes about conventional musicals is that "one minute the characters are talking, the next minute they're singing; and a moment later, they're talking again." So he and Steven

Sater (book and lyrics) conceived their songs as "interior monologues", voicing "the thoughts and feelings of each character's private landscape". Fine. But why, then, in their "private landscapes" do these repressed Wilhelmine Germans become twenty-first century Americans, vaulting round the stage like *American Idol* auditionees, emoting in the language of MTV, complete with anachronistic references to stereos and telephones? The answer, I presume, is that they are meant to embody the timeless tribulations of adolescence. Yet ever and again the structure militates against that.

We have a scene of Prussian authoritarianism in the schoolroom where boys chant Latin and are beaten by their masters for minor infractions, something so remote from the atmosphere of a modern American high school that the gorge rises when the boys whip microphones out of their high-collared jackets and launch into a heavy-rock anthem, 'The Bitch of Living' – *"this is so not life at all."* Are they historically determined figures or are they timeless avatars of adolescence? The authors seemed unsure. In one interview composer Sheik said that "these are children who ultimately are going to be parents of Nazis." Meanwhile lyricist Sater told another interviewer that rock music is "the place where kids for generations have found release from unformed anguish." Well, correct me if I'm wrong but I don't recall rock music playing a decisive role in the rise of Nazism.

Or take the opening scene. In the play, Wedekind constructs this very carefully to introduce his theme of adult hypocrisy. We have what at first sight looks like a 'modern' situation. A daughter is arguing with her mother over the length of her dress – the girl wants it short, the mother says it's too short. So far, so 1966 (*et seq*). But, unlike her miniskirted descendant, Wendla isn't laying claim to some 'teenage' fashion; she isn't carving out a special peer identity to distinguish herself from the parent generation. She wants to remain a child and doesn't want to be an adult if it means wearing long dresses. The mother tells her daughter it's time to adopt adult clothes but, as we learn in a later scene where she deflects questions about pregnancy, isn't prepared to arm Wendla with the information she will need to function as an adult. This dialogue is truncated in the musical script and we move into Wendla's "private landscape" where she sings 'Mama who bore me', even though the text will establish that the girl has no idea where babies come from.

Still, what do I know? The night I saw the show (at the Lyric Hammersmith) the audience was packed with young people who seemed to be enjoying every minute of it. The young principals were excellent and the choreography (by Bill T Jones) was stupendous. Heck, I even liked some of the songs. I'm sure *Spring Awakening* could make great musical theatre. All Wedekind's plays leave room for music. With his anti-naturalist style, there are always jagged edges that could be smoothed, gaps between scenes and styles that could fill with music. But probably not *this* music. In its ambition it reminded me of Christina Paulhofer's production of *Franziska* (Staatsschauspielhaus, Hannover, 2003) – where Wedekind's baggy original was rewritten by Thea Dorn as an elaborate pop theatre spectacle of mixed styles; yet somehow the Germans do these things more convincingly.

Sondheim at 90

[Written in March 2020. Sadly, the composer-lyricist, something of a personal hero of mine, would see only one more birthday. He died on 26 November 2021.]

The Grand Old Man of the American musical turns 90 this weekend. Many, many happy returns to him. Whether the show he's said to be currently engaged on – based around two Buñuel movies – will ever see the light of day is a moot point. I'm not alone among Sondheim fans in sensing a falling-off in quality in his output over the last twenty-five years, so I'm not holding my breath. But prior to *Passion* (1994), his last work of importance, there was already a lifetime of achievement to celebrate.

Sondheim must be the only significant figure still active in musical theatre to have come of age before the rock'n'roll revolution. His musical sensibilities were formed in the late 1940s and early '50s. It was an age of professional song-writers and of performers beholden to them. In later decades these separate roles would fuse: artists, generally unversed in musical staff notation, would originate, record and perform their own material, often working it up in the studio (as The Beatles did after their retreat from public performance in 1966). These developments largely passed Sondheim by. Pop or rock has only ever featured in a 'diegetic' sense in his shows. In 'Unworthy of Your Love' (from *Assassins*, 1990) he creates a soppy Carpenters-like ballad to characterize 'Squeaky' Fromme, would-be assassin of President Ford, because *that's the sort of music she would have listened to*. The writer David Benedict is working on a new biography of Sondheim. After the reappearance of photos from the late '60s showing Sondheim chilling with the 'Bronx Madonna', Laura Nyro, I asked David about Sondheim and later currents in American music. He replied:

… Obviously, he has always been aware of music that surrounded him, like the singer-songwriter movement of the 1960s and '70s, but he was and always has been a theatre writer. He's really not interested in songs disconnected from drama. He listens to orchestral/classical music on a daily basis – the more arcane, the better since his knowledge of the standard classical repertoire is genuinely encyclopaedic – but next to no contemporary 'pop' (for want of a better term) music, unless occasionally persuaded by others.

My first Sondheim experience was the anthology show *Side by Side by Sondheim* (1976).[18] I recall a TV discussion between the man himself and a suave, roll-necked André Previn which prompted me to book for the original London production, and I still play the cast album a lot. The two-piano arrangements brought out the subtlety of his harmonies better than the pit orchestras and scaled-down orchestrations that one is likely to encounter in productions beyond the West End. And in Julia McKenzie, Millicent Martin and David Kernan you had three of Sondheim's best interpreters on this side of the pond. After that I went on to explore the individual shows, first tracking down the original cast albums, then catching productions when they

---

[18] More accurately, my first *conscious* Sondheim experience. As a child I was taken to see the film of *A Funny Thing Happened on the Way to the Forum* (1966) and retained the tune of 'Comedy Tonight' in memory. It was only when I heard the opening number of *Side by Side by Sondheim* a decade later that I made the connection.

landed in London or other English cities.

For me, his masterpiece is *Sweeney Todd* (1979). Much as I love the other shows, especially those from his peak of creativity in the 1970s, I have reservations about many of them, either about the concept or because the thing just didn't work for me on stage. *Company* (1970), in which a group of Manhattanites attempt to marry off their bachelor friend, becomes more believable in its gender-swapped reworking of recent years; I still found the songs more interesting than the characters who sing them. *Pacific Overtures* (1976) was a bold attempt to narrate the opening up of Japan to the West by fusing Broadway with *kabuki*: it's desperately clever but I found it cold and lacking in focus on individual characters. In a couple of later shows – *Sunday in the Park with George* (1984) and *Into the Woods* (1987) – he and his writing partner use the device of apparently bringing resolution at the end of Act One, only to unpick it again after the interval: a high-risk strategy. *Sweeney* has none of these weaknesses: a strong story with a classic narrative arc; characters who burst the bonds of caricature; an inventive, near through-composed score; genuine frights, relieved by black humour. People took against Hal Prince's original production, in which the *grand guignol* of Todd's vendetta was played out on a huge set representing Victorian industrialisation. I, however, thought it was inspired: it universalised the barber's predicament without sacrificing his homicidal particularity. 'The Musical of the Outsider' is how Jim Lovensheimer titles his chapter on Sondheim for *The Cambridge Companion to the Musical*. "He seems always to have been attracted to characters whose actions place them outside mainstream society." Although Lovensheimer concentrates his discussion on the misfits of *Assassins* who "can't get in to the ball park," there is no outsider more archetypal than the Demon Barber of Fleet Street.

"Taking a line for a walk" – Paul Klee's memorable description of drawing comes to mind when I think of Sondheim's lyrics. Words falling into place with an apparent effortlessness that one can only inspire awe in anyone who's ever struggled to write words for singing, words that go to unexpected places but with secure locomotion on two steady feet. Take the saucy little number 'Can That Boy Foxtrot', written for *Follies* (1971) but later cut (one of many examples of Sondheim outtakes that are at least as good as the songs that stayed in). We're left in no doubt where this grocery clerk's special talents lie:

His mouth is mean,
He's not too clean,
What makes him look reptilian
Is the brilliantine.
But oh,
Can that boy f..oxtrot!

As dumbbells go,
He's rather slow
And as for being saintly,
Even faintly, no,
But who needs Albert Schweitzer
When the lights're low,
And oh boy, oh boy,
Can that boy... foxtrot!

The rhymes are never gratuitous, they speed the line, they point up the joke. No wonder actors and singers love performing this stuff. Vowel length and colour, consonant choices are never left to chance. Check out the TV master-class (1984) in which Sondheim takes a student through 'My Friends', the rhapsodic ode in *Sweeney Todd* where the barber is reunited with the tools of his trade. The lyric starts with an accumulation of sibilants; the barber is whispering sweet-nothings to his razor. Then he opens out onto a vowel when he reaches the title words, his mania rising as the melodic line rises.

Sondheim claims he is not a great reader, more of a movie buff. This has always surprised me since his lyrics exhibit such passion for language. But perhaps it's the passion of the crossword-compiler, the professional puzzle-setter – two activities he has engaged in in the past. Indeed, the shows are often about setting himself puzzles, the more difficult the better. In *A Little Night Music* (1973) the challenge was to compose an entire score in triple-time metres; in *Merrily We Roll Along* (1981) the story unfolds in reverse, its characters moving from disillusioned middle age to wide-eyed youth over the course of the show, a development mirrored musically as songs are heard in their 'final' form near the beginning, then in embryonic form later in the score.

Sondheim's work is the antithesis of the 'jukebox' musical which now dominates in London and New York. In this genre the trick is to take an existing catalogue – songs already known to the theatre audience but not written for the theatre – devise a plot that can be plausibly punctuated by the songs you've chosen, assign songs to the characters you've created and then stage the show. Fair play: I yield to none in admiration for the ABBA songbook, and *Mamma Mia!* is a glorious romp, but it lacks most of the qualities I appreciate in Sondheim. By contrast, he writes for character, each song tailored to the dramatic circumstances of its place in the show, with the result that few of his songs have prospered outside the work they were written for. Even his only 'hit', 'Send in the Clowns', has a contextual meaning which is lost when the song floats free from the original show. In *A Little Night Music* it is sung by the middle-aged actress Desirée reflecting on the disappointments of her life. When Judy Collins delivered the song on *The Muppet Show* she was memorably surrounded by dancing clowns. All wrong. Too literal, as Sondheim explained in a 1990 interview:

I wanted to use theatrical imagery in the song, because she's an actress, but it's not supposed to be a circus [...] It's a theatre reference meaning "if the show isn't going well, let's send in the clowns"; in other words, "let's do the jokes."

He dislikes reprises – if a character sings her first-act song unchanged in Act Two it means she hasn't undergone any development in between. No reprises, no chance to ram the melody into the audience's heads and send them whistling out of the theatre. There *are* 'earworms' in Sondheim, but they take time to insinuate themselves. To those who say he can't write 'tunes', I say, go investigate *Liaisons*, a remarkable three-disc set from 2015. Pianist Anthony de Mare commissioned thirty-six contemporary composers each to 're-imagine' a Sondheim song as a piano piece. The variety of music they spin out of the Sondheim originals shows how fruitful his 'tunes' can be. In 'Johanna', Duncan Sheik (whose own musical *Spring Awakening* comes from a very different place) leaves the source material relatively unchanged but layers dozens of takes of guitar improvisation through a tape echo, "creating a blanket of sound for the piano to linger within". Steve Reich's arrangement of 'Finishing the Hat' for two pianos gives us Sondheim the minimalist. Wynton Marsalis's 'That Old Piano Roll' is a romp through different jazz piano styles, while Mark-Anthony Turnage paraphrases 'Pretty Women' to dissolve the song into its emotional components. Sondheim's distinctive compositional technique of using short motifs as structural cells for lengthier statements almost invites this sort of 're-imagining'.

Classically trained in music, Sondheim studied composition with Milton Babbitt, most uncompromising of American serialists. His musical language remains distinctively his own, although an early enthusiasm for Ravel often breaks through (his undergraduate thesis was on Ravel's Piano Concerto for the Left Hand). Like Ravel he delights in unobvious harmonic choices – ninths, elevenths, thirteenths abound – and like the French master he is a fastidious craftsman, skilled in pastiching other styles while retaining the integrity of his own voice.

Of course, musicals are a true collaborative art, and Sondheim has always emphasised that his shows wouldn't exist without their 'book', the spoken dialogue supplied by another writer. But the fact that he combines the functions of composer and lyricist, roles which are conventionally separated, makes for an unusually tight fit, an unusual degree of coherence across his body of work. I've lived with this body of work now for forty years or more and return to it often, whether as listener, theatre-goer or as inept amateur pianist, stumbling through his tricky accompaniments and hitting another wrong note. My own musical tastes are eclectic; in fantasy I picture myself as some sort of bridge-builder between discrete genres. Sondheim shows how you can take a commercially driven, 'popular' form like the musical and raise it to a 'high' art. 'Art isn't easy' – as one of his artist characters sings – but it is possible. Happy birthday, Mr Sondheim!

Mitford Connections

There is no escaping the Mitford mythology. Those six well-bred sisters (and the brother no one talks about much) who romanced more than a little when the topic was themselves, and romanced themselves into our lives, where they've taken up residence ever since. Sometime at the start of the Eighties, when I was living in London, I saw a small ad in *Time Out*, the capital's listings magazine: "Musical theatre lyricist seeks composer with view to collaboration" (or words to that effect). Some imp on my shoulder prompted me to reply. I had one short meeting with this budding Hammerstein, who rapidly saw through me. He arrived with an impressive set of lyrics for an adaptation of an Oscar Wilde story.[19] All I had to offer was a rough outline of *Unity! The Musical* and a few mouldy-cheesy melodies. "Extraordinary how potent cheap music is," I suggested, quoting – to no avail – a line of Noël Coward he was sure to recognise. "Yes… I'm sorry we can't work together," he said as he took his leave. "Have you thought of writing film music?"

Unity! (the exclamation mark was essential, as in *Oliver!*) would tell the story of Unity Mitford, battiest of all the sisterhood. While her sister Jessica espoused Communism and another sister, Diana, married Oswald

---

[19] I wish I could remember *which* Oscar Wilde story. I like to think it was 'The Portrait of Mr W. H.', because that would create a pleasing red thread back to an earlier essay in this volume. Let's say it was.

Mosley, Unity moved to Germany and insinuated herself into Hitler's circle. The Führer took a shine to her, even as he disapproved of her heavy make-up, so different from the fresh-faced Aryan ideal. With her family's social connections she might be a conduit to high-born Nazi-sympathisers in England, perhaps even to Edward VIII (later Duke of Windsor). Alternatively, she might be a spy, an unlikely 'honey-trap'. Questions were asked back home about her traitorous conduct. When Britain declared war on Germany in 1939, the poor mooncalf's loyalties were fatally divided and she attempted to take her own life. Surviving, but with health much impaired, she was invalided back to Britain where she lived out her remaining days in the care of her family (not before – if you believe one of the loopier conspiracy theories attaching to her story – giving birth in secret to Hitler's love-child).

My starting point was her sister Jessica's provocative notion that there were good haters and bad haters, and Unity as she grew up passed from one camp to the other. Jessica wrote in her autobiography, *Hons and Rebels*:

[Unity] was always a terrific hater... but I had always thought she hated intelligently, and admired her ability to reduce the more unpleasant of the grown-up relations to a state of acute nervous discomfort with one of her smouldering looks of loathing. But when she wrote gaily off to *Der Stürmer*, "I want everybody to know I am a Jew-hater", I felt she had forgotten the whole point of hating, and had once and for all put herself on the side of the hateful.

Dark, uncompromising material for a musical. Is hatred itself ever anything but hateful? How can we not but hate the person who hates? Can we 'understand' them? I imagined *Unity!* as something between *Cabaret* and *Sweeney Todd*. But in the hands of an inexperienced apprentice writer, the results were likely to be closer to *Springtime for Hitler*, Mel Brooks's classic spoof of The Musical From Hell. In any case, seasoned professionals were already all over the subject. 1981 saw a BBC TV adaptation of David Pryce-Jones's biography of Unity (with Lesley-Anne Down in the title role and Derek Jacobi as Hitler). And in the same year a musical, *The Mitford Girls*, opened at the Chichester Festival Theatre, later transferring to the West End. Written by the established team of Caryl Brahms and Ned Sherrin, with a tinkly Twenties-style score by Peter Greenwell, this show ventured to give only one number to Unity:

Strange forces cloud our skies
Pulling us apart.
Strange sadness clouds our eyes,
Heavy is the heart...

The weighty implications of Unity's story were sidestepped. Nothing to frighten the horses here. A few years later Stephen Sondheim produced one of his darkest musicals, *Assassins*, a show about presidential assassins and would-be assassins. Maybe this was how you put messed-up people with hate in their hearts on the musical theatre stage? The show opened off-Broadway in 1990 to decidedly mixed reviews, but later revivals have confirmed its honesty in confronting the flipside of the American Dream.

Unity! The Musical may yet see the light of day. Recent innovations in music software have put some smart kit into the hands of even the most inept tunesmiths; I feel the loins of compositional impotence begin to stir again after many years. Goodness knows what became of the Oscar Wilde man, my not-to-be collaborator: I don't see his name emblazoned across the West End. So I may have to be my own lyricist (there are fine precedents).

***

A hundred years ago, the 17-year-old Nancy Mitford was in Florence on a cultural tour with four other girls, chaperoned by a Miss Spalding. A highlight of the trip was going to see an Italian movie. She calls it 'Dante', but it must have been the 1911 film *L'Inferno*, which corresponds to the very detailed description she gives in a letter home to her mother.[20] It was a surprising choice for a group of schoolgirls. "I never saw anything like it before, it was enough to make you dream for nights," wrote Nancy. Hardly surprising: it doesn't hold back on the violence and nudity. She says the showing lasted from 9 pm to 12.15 with two intervals. They must have been long intervals, given that the film's running time appears in reference books as around 1 hour 11 minutes. Perhaps the audience needed time to recover between reels? Nancy, unshaken, found it "most bloodthirsty & exciting"; the devils reminded her of those drawn by her sister Unity. Dark shadows haunted even the perennially upbeat Nancy.

***

I am also intrigued by one of the outliers, a figure on the edges of the Mitford family saga who has received little attention. The six famous sisters had, albeit briefly, a German-Jewish aunt. She was rarely spoken of, and while Nancy might have found the connection amusing, it would have been anathema to Unity or Diana. This was Marie-Anne, also known as Marianne, who married into the family in 1914, and just as swiftly exited from it. The story of her

---

[20] *The Letters of Nancy Mitford*, ed. Charlotte Mosley, 17 April 1922.

marriage to Uncle Jack and of the different paths the couple took after their parting is worth the telling.

Marie-Anne von Friedländer-Fuld (b. 1892) was the only child of the Berlin 'Coal King', Privy Councillor Friedrich von Friedländer-Fuld. Her father, a self-made industrialist who dominated the Berlin coal market, was reckoned by the *New York Times* to be worth in excess of $11 million, and steward of an even larger fortune his daughter stood to inherit. Friedrich, it was reported, was among the men on whom the Kaiser depended financially for his "patriotic schemes". Although Marianne's ancestry on both the father's and mother's side was Jewish, the family had converted to Christianity and was ennobled by the Kaiser in 1906. The family's palatial home on the Pariser Platz near the Brandenburg Gate was a social hub, and the young heiress did not lack for suitors. Newspapers trilled that she was a "beautiful brunette", an accomplished linguist and a fearless horsewoman, whose earlier engagement to a cousin of the Tsar had been thwarted only when Nicholas II learned of her Jewish parentage. Known to her friends as 'Baby', she was also a discerning art collector, with an eye for Impressionists and other modern masters. By 1914 she had already acquired at least one valuable asset in a Van Gogh portrait, 'L'Arlésienne' (of which more later).

The Hon. John Mitford (b. 1885), known as 'Jack' or 'Jicksy' within the family, was cut from rather different cloth. Reportedly the favourite among his father's five sons, he is described in *The House of Mitford* as a "charming scapegrace" and a "rolling stone" who was "well known in the family for being a card". Expelled from Eton, he'd been unable to enter the diplomatic service for which his father had destined him. He instead chose banking as a career, moving to France in 1907, ostensibly to learn Continental business practices, then to Germany. From 1910 to 1913 he was engaged in private banking for Warburg in Hamburg. He met Marianne at the Kiel Regatta – probably introduced by their mutual friend, Admiral Prince Henry of Prussia, the Kaiser's younger brother and Patron of the Kiel Yacht Club – and proposed. According to David Pryce-Jones, whose grandfather attended the wedding, the marriage was Prince Henry's idea: a misfiring attempt at Anglo-German alliance. In addition to gifting the couple a luxurious house in the Bendlerstrasse, as part of the marriage settlement Friedrich von Friedländer-Fuld made his new English son-in-law a partner in the family business – unkind souls suggested in order to ensure the accumulated wealth was likely to remain in Germany. It was reportedly a condition of the marriage contract that the couple were not to reside entirely in England. Whatever expectations the contracting parties brought to the table, the wedding was bound to be the highlight of the Berlin social calendar in early 1914.

Celebrations began with the 'Polterabend', the traditional eve-of-wedding ball, on 4 January, a spectacular affair. In a room which was an exact replica of Frederick the Great's Concert Room at Sans Souci, a company of 300 sat down to dinner. Once the tables had been cleared, aristocratic eyebrows were raised when the tango was danced, the Kaiser having decreed that the tango was strictly forbidden at houses frequented by Army officers or members of Court society. Music was provided by the 'Philharmonic Orchestra' (presumably the Berlin Philharmonic?) and the evening ended with live drama. Max Reinhardt brought members of his Deutsches Theater troupe to act scenes from *A Midsummer Night's Dream*, with Gertrud Eysoldt as Puck and Alexander Moissi as Oberon, and there was an exhibition dance by Grete Wiesenthal, one of the leading exponents of 'modern dance' in Germany at the time.

After a civil ceremony the following day, the service at Trinity Church on 6 January 1914 followed Lutheran rites. Guests numbered ambassadors, Prussian ministers, military brasshats (including Moltke, Chief of the General Staff) and the most prominent Berlin families – though, not it seems, any members of the Imperial Family, who pleaded a prior engagement. The wedding broke with German precedent, for it had hitherto been custom at society weddings to wear evening dress, however early in the day. In deference to the bridegroom's nationality, the dress code was 'English', i.e. morning dress. The bride was in white satin, with a veil of old Silesian lace. In his address, the pastor noted the coincidence that this union of Redesdale and Friedländer-Fuld families was forged "at a time when Anglo-German political friendship was increasing" and urged the young couple to fill their house "not only with material things but with the Anglo-German spirit". It was a spirit that would not survive the year, on either the personal or the international level.

What happened next is a matter of conjecture, not least since both families made efforts to hush the matter up. When the honeymooners returned from six weeks on the Riviera, something was awry. Although Lady Redesdale was able to present her new daughter-in-law to King George and Queen Mary at Court on 13 March (Marianne wearing her much-admired wedding dress), within another month it was known that 'Baby' had decided to live apart from her husband. Jack returned to England, Baby to her parents' home, and the house prepared for the couple on the Bendlerstrasse was left temporarily unoccupied. Rumours circulated in Berlin that the cause of separation was "unnatural conduct on the part of Mr Mitford". This gossip was picked up by *The Sporting Times* in London and ill-advisedly repeated in an article in July. The paper didn't refer to the Mitfords by name, but only by inference after linking their story to that of another married couple. Still, this was enough for Jack to launch a libel action against the paper. In an affidavit he attested that he had lived an "absolutely clean life" and there was "not an atom of truth in the abominable suggestion" in the article. In his eyes, the couple were "perfectly happy". His wife, he said, had become ill in May and entered a sanatorium. On his second visit to her there, she had informed him they were "unsuited". He couldn't account for her "strange and sudden determination" but believed it to be only temporary. As evidence that she was still "full of affection" for him, he produced a letter she'd written to his mother, Lady Redesdale. The letter's tone is certainly conciliatory – but perhaps disingenuous, given the legal action she was contemplating in Germany to end the marriage. She apologises for "the pain I am giving your beloved son" and assures her mother-in-law that Jack "never wronged anyone"; nevertheless, since the couple "lived away from one another inwardly," she insisted there had to be a parting of the ways.

For some reason, Jack had gone down a precarious legal route. Under English law at the time, prosecutions by private individuals could be begun by 'criminal information' as well as by indictment. However, individuals had to obtain the leave of the court to file an information. A case in 1884 had already decided that there would be a presumption against granting this right to private individuals as distinct from someone in public office. (Indeed, 'criminal informations' were abolished in

1938.) In Jack's case, the Lord Chief Justice opined that while the paragraph complained of undoubtedly contained "matter of a grave character," he didn't consider it grounds for a criminal information, given that Jack was not a holder of public office.

Thus he had only succeeded in drawing his marital problems into the public arena. Baby remained fixed in her determination to end the marriage and in June 1914 petitioned the German court on the grounds that Jack was "addicted to masculine indolence and unbearable selfishness". She successfully invoked a curious provision in the German Civil Code which allowed a spouse to dispute the validity of a marriage if either party was "mistaken as to the personal attributes of the other spouse" at the time of the marriage. The court, finding in her favour, declared the marriage null and void in October 1914. Jack was not best pleased. He instructed his lawyers in Germany to refute the charges against him. However, after the outbreak of war in August, he couldn't communicate with them directly and was unable to give evidence in person. His counsel appealed twice on his behalf in 1916 – ultimately to the Imperial Supreme Court – but the higher courts upheld the original decision.

We know all this from reports of another court case initiated by Jack in the English courts, which seems to have been as ill-starred as his earlier libel action. Marianne had remarried in 1920, to the diplomat Richard von Kühlmann. In March 1921, Jack, who still regarded her as his lawful wife, petitioned the High Court in London for dissolution of his marriage on the grounds of Baby's alleged bigamy and adultery with Kühlmann. The English court found – predictably, one would have thought – that since the dissolution of the first marriage and the contracting of

Marianne's second took place in Germany under German law, the English court had no jurisdiction. The ground of 'mistaken identity', though it would be immaterial in English law, was valid under German.

But this is jumping ahead. To revert to the events of autumn 1914... At the outbreak of war Jack did not wait to be conscripted but immediately joined the Life Guards, to serve with the British Expeditionary Force in France. The empty marital home in Berlin was used at first to house East Prussian refugees before welcoming a more illustrious resident at year's end. Marianne had met the poet Rainer Maria Rilke at a funeral in November. An invitation to tea followed and Rilke was soon a regular visitor at her parents' home to which she had now retreated. Hearing that Rilke was in need of accommodation, she offered him rooms in the half-vacant Bendlerstrasse house. He moved in before Christmas. "She is a marvellously beautiful creature," he wrote later, "who, emerging from childhood of which she still bears the dark traces, had suddenly been transformed by a touch of fate into an independent limpid personality, transparent through and through." She became one of his closest confidantes and throughout the war, when far from Berlin, Rilke honoured her with lengthy letters drawing on their shared passion for art in which, as his biographer puts it, a "faint hint of the erotic was always overlaid by his didacticism and self-preoccupation."

The death of Marianne's father in July 1917 left her a very rich woman. In 1922 she became a limited partner in the family firm, a position she held until 1936 when Nazi race laws forced the exclusion of Jewish staff and the confiscation of family assets. The marriage to Kühlmann which so exercised Jack's litigious instincts was short-lived. After the birth of a daughter, Antoinette, they divorced in

1923. She then married the painter Rudolf von Goldschmidt-Rothschild. Marrying this time into an observant family, she returned to Judaism. A son, Gilbert, was born in 1925. As a refined Berlin *salonnière* she flits across the pages of diarists in the 1920s. The artistic patron Count Harry Kessler was one such. He records her taste for amateur dramatics (at one *soirée* she improvises a parody of a play by Hugo von Hofmannsthal, causing Kessler, one of Hofmannsthal's closest friends, to see the hollowness of a work he once revered). He visits her one afternoon in 1926: "She received me in bed, between pink damask sheets and in blue pyjamas, the Chinese bed upholstered in yellow satin. A setting appropriate to the bedroom scene in a play about adultery." Three years later, after she hosts an intimate dinner party, thirty Van Gogh letters in an "excessively ornate, ugly binding" are handed round with cigarettes and coffee. Kessler starts to fret that acquisitiveness may have got the better of connoisseurship. "Poor Van Gogh!" he muses to his diary, disgusted at the "falsification and degradation of intellectual and artistic values to mere baubles, 'luxurious' possessions."

Entering the 1930s, she was increasingly exercised by the plight of German Jewry. It was said that, after the passing of the Nuremberg Laws, she took (in defiance?) to wearing a Star of David of yellow diamonds. In September 1936 Winston Churchill, returning from one of his painting holidays on the Côte d'Azur, dined with her in Toulon and heard early hints of an unfolding horror in Europe. He wrote to his wife Clementine that Marianne was a remarkable woman who had told him "terrible" tales of the treatment of Jews in Germany.

Like the two before it, the marriage to Goldschmidt-Rothschild did not last, and Marianne was once more a divorcee when she fled Germany in October 1938. She emigrated first to France, before making her way in 1940, via Spain, Portugal and Mexico, to the USA, where she sat out the remainder of the war. Accompanying her were the two children from two marriages and some of the precious artworks, including the Van Gogh. On returning to Europe in the late Forties, she sought restitution of property and assets, with partial success. She published her letters from Rilke (in French translation) in 1956 under the pseudonym 'Marianne Gilbert'. As for 'L'Arlésienne', she vowed that when Paris was liberated she would donate the canvas to the French nation: following her death in 1973 it hangs now in the Musée d'Orsay.

Jack, for his part, never remarried. After his failed lawsuit in the early Twenties, he seems to have accepted that Baby was lost to him. Pryce-Jones describes him in later life as "a somewhat Ivor-Novello-model of a bobbish man about town" and the inspiration behind the International Sportsman's Club in Grosvenor House. He was secretary of the Marlborough Club and a regular visitor and competitor at St Moritz for the Cresta Run, where he was pictured with various photogenic young women, including Sheilah Graham, the upwardly mobile Englishwoman who would go on to have an affair with Scott Fitzgerald. A photo spread in the *Tatler* in 1933 captures Unity and Deborah Mitford on the ski slopes watching their "adored Uncle Jack" compete in the Curzon Cup. He made headlines briefly in February 1940 after Unity had been invalided out of Germany following her suicide attempt, telling reporters he "did not credit the theory" that his niece's bullet wound was self-inflicted. Thus are conspiracy theories born. (Several months after this George Orwell records in his diary the rumour that Unity was pregnant by the Führer – another *canard* that continues to resurface to this day.) In his final years Jack was looked after by his unmarried sister Iris. He inherited the barony from his childless older brother Bertram in 1962, to become the fourth Baron Redesdale, but died only a year later; as Jack was also without issue, the title passed to his nephew Clement.

Perhaps it was all there in the wedding photo. A slightly Bertie-Woosterish bridegroom inclines towards a serene bride, her gaze fixed straight ahead. An older lady (the bride's mother?) looks on sceptically, wondering if it will last. An affable, sporty English gentleman, none too bright, whose pleasures were skiing and sailing, weds a cultured German socialite with a compensating social conscience, at ease among poets and artists. Add in the fissures of nationality and race that ran through their troubled era. The outlook was never good for this particular Anglo-German alliance.

[Principal sources: *The Times* Law Reports; *New York Times*; Jonathan and Catherine Guinness, *The House of Mitford: Portrait of a Family* (1984); David Pryce-Jones, *Unity Mitford: A Quest* (1976); Donald Prater, *A Ringing Glass: The Life of Rainer Maria Rilke* (1986); Count Harry Kessler, *The Diaries of a Cosmopolitan, 1918-1937* (1971); Marianne Gilbert, *Le tiroir entr'ouvert* (1956).]

(With thanks to Lyndsy Spence and The Mitford Society.)

Myth: Its Manufacture and Recovery

Anthropologists and classicists speculate about how myths came into being in pre-literate cultures. My interest is rather in the creation and re-creation of myth in historical time, a process which lends itself to more exact study. There can be few better places to focus that study than the German-speaking lands in the late nineteenth and early twentieth centuries. George Eliot, most cosmopolitan of Victorian novelists, anticipated as much when she wrote *Middlemarch* (1872). In that novel the leathery old clergyman Mr Casaubon is engaged in lifelong research for his *magnum opus*, the *Key to All Mythologies*. It is fruitless work, "mouldy futilities" – so his wife is assured by young Will Ladislaw – because he does not read German. Without that language Casaubon cannot keep up with the new scholarship in comparative religion and mythology, fields in which Germany led the world.

Central to the German preoccupation with myth was the belief that it was somehow 'original', 'living' and authentic. Uses of myth in the modern period therefore claim to be restorative of lost traditions; in fact, they are more often 'inventions of tradition' (in Eric Hobsbawm's phrase). Are they, then, to be judged as massive delusional systems? Or are we looking at a transformation of 'myth' into something more appropriate to a mass culture?

One place to start is the relationship between myth and history as the debate was conducted in the late nineteenth century among German classicists. How do they gloss the definition of *muthos* in Plato and Aristotle, and Herodotus's use of 'unhistorical' evidence? Is the resurgent interest in myth a reaction against Positivism and the Rankean view of history? This might lead one to consideration of Nietzsche's assault on the philological profession and his deliberations on myth (*The Birth of Tragedy*) and history (*On the Uses and Disadvantages of History for Life*).

Nietzsche attended the laying of the foundation stone of the Bayreuth Festspielhaus in 1872, at which time he still believed that a rebirth of tragedy could be effected through Wagnerian music-drama. It would be interesting to follow through the concept of the *Festspiel* – understood as an attempted renewal of the 'Volk' through communal theatre on mythical subjects – down to Wagner's heirs at the turn of the century: Appia and Jacques-Dalcroze in Hellerau, Georg Fuchs in Munich and Count Kessler in Weimar. How important was it that each of these attempts was under-written by aristocratic patronage, beginning with Ludwig II's support of Wagner?

Ludwig's cousin, Elisabeth of Austria, offers a case-study in the creation of personal myth, which brought her into conflict with official Habsburg ideology. During her lifetime Elisabeth controlled her own iconography by taking advantage of the new medium of photography. After her death biographical myths accreted around her which continue to be influential to this day, as the buoyant 'Sisi' industry in Austria demonstrates. The Empress united in her person Romantic Hellenism and identification with figures from Greek mythology, especially that of Persephone.

Arnold Böcklin's painting *The Island of the Dead* (1880) strongly evokes Elisabeth's beloved retreat of Corfu. A survey of the decline of 'history painting' in nineteenth-century Germany (pivoting around the Symbolist art of Böcklin) might ask whether there is a point where shared mythologies collapse and private ones take their place. A thin line leads by way of Makart and Anselm Feuerbach to the paintings of early Expressionism.

Böcklin's Leonardo-like experimentation with flying machines and Max Beckmann's monumental canvas *The Sinking of the 'Titanic'* (painted 1912) exemplify the instant mythologization of history. German responses to the 'Titanic' disaster have received little attention from scholars: a comparison with other accidents – airship and aeroplane crashes – suggests that the process of mythologization operates particularly where classically-minded observers believe they are witnessing the latest technology brought low by its own *hubris* (in the manner of a tragic hero).

By giving a blood transfusion to certain received myths, notably that of Oedipus ("blood for the ghosts", in Nietzsche's memorable phrase), Sigmund Freud ensured their survival as 'general knowledge'. The reciprocal relation between Freud's classical learning and his medical practice is a fascinating subject. When he adopted a Greek myth as an explanatory tool for a psychoanalytic theory, which came first, the myth or the clinical diagnosis?

There are striking similarities between Freud's thought and that of Johann Jakob Bachofen (1815-1887). Largely neglected in the English-speaking world, Bachofen was hugely influential on German-speaking intellectuals when his work was reissued in the 1920s. Thomas Mann (*Joseph and His Brothers*), Ernst Krenek (the opera *Life of Orestes*) and the painter Oskar Kokoschka all drew inspiration from Bachofen's argument that we can reconstruct unwritten prehistory through the study of myth; but they reversed his intentions, seeking to reanimate myth by turning the 'facts' supposedly preserved by myth back into the 'fiction' of art.

Thomas Mann's criticisms of Alfred Baeumler, editor of the 1926 edition of Bachofen, led directly to his conviction that psychology offered the best means to rescue myth from Fascism ('Freud and the Future', 1936). The precariousness of that hope is illustrated through Leni Riefenstahl's film *Triumph of the Will* (1934). Here present, put to equivocal use, are so many aspects of the manufacture of myth – the cultic coming-together of the 'Volk' at a great 'Fest' (the Party rally), the romance of technology (as in the opening shot of the Führer's plane descending, Valkyrie-like, through the clouds), the manipulation of image (tension between the director's editorial control and that of the Party, mirroring the film's troubled status somewhere between art and propaganda).

So, a question for any latterday Will Ladislaws out there: is it possible to recover the originally progressive intentions of the Romantic concept of myth? From the plenitude of Greek myth I pick out three examples that have always fascinated me...

Anyone who has grappled with *The Waste Land*, that foundation document of literary Modernism, will have made their way to the Notes at the end. Here, T.S. Eliot comes to the aid of "any who think... elucidation of the poem worth the trouble" by listing some of his sources. His note to line 218 suggests that "Tiresias, although a mere spectator and not indeed a 'character', is yet the most important personage in the poem, uniting all the rest". All the women mentioned in the poem, he continues, "are one woman, and the two sexes meet in Tiresias. What Tiresias sees, in fact, is the substance of the poem." Eliot's note concludes with a lengthy quotation (in Latin) from Ovid.

The tale of the Theban seer **Tiresias** appears in Book III of Ovid's *Metamorphoses*. Ovid relates how Tiresias once saw two snakes mating, struck them with his staff and was changed into a woman. Seven years later he saw them and hit them again, causing him to revert to man's shape. Some time after his sex changes he was called upon to settle a dispute between Zeus and Hera on whether men or women get more pleasure from sex, he having experienced both. He declared for women, in a ratio of nine to one. Hera, out of spite, struck him blind but Zeus compensated him with the gift of unerring prophecy.

One of my favourite definitions of myth is one I came across in the writings of the French classicist Jean-Pierre Vernant. He understood myth as implying a union of opposites, a means of bringing into play "shifts, slides, tensions and oscillations between the very terms that are distinguished or opposed in [the story's] categorical framework."[21] Understood thus, the Tiresias myth becomes a kind of exemplar. It frames a question that Tiresias alone can answer. "Throbbing between two lives," as Eliot describes him in *The Waste Land*, he alone knows whether we experience the world differently if our 'identity' changes. A pertinent question in an age of 'identitarianism'.

The Tiresias myth also attracted the French poet and dramatist Guillaume Apollinaire. His play *Les Mamelles de Tirésias*, first performed in 1917 is best known through its operatic adaptation by Francis Poulenc. However, I think there are good reasons for reviving the original, which was a *succès de scandale* in its time, and I once tried to persuade a theatre director to that point of view. The play has never had a professional production in London, as far as I'm aware.

---

[21] *Myth and Society in Ancient Greece*, tr. Janet Lloyd (1979).

Les Mamelles is wonderfully anarchic, full of strange events and juxtapositions. It tilts at militarism, gender roles, journalism, love, marriage, parenthood, and just about every other serious subject. Death means nothing – characters simply get up again after being shot with cardboard guns. Greek myth is subverted when the seer Tiresias is portrayed as a bearded lady with balloons for breasts. In his po-faced preface to the play (where he makes early use of the word "surrealism", which he coined), Apollinaire claims that *Les Mamelles* is about the "population" question (the declining birth rate). But one suspects that this is a cipher for the more intriguing question of "where do babies come from?" The language is extravagant, with frequent disarming shifts of register. In a Prologue, the "Director" links his experiences in the trenches of the First World War with the need for a new theatre, shorn of outdated expectations. Perhaps this could form a double bill with something by one of Apollinaire's heirs, say Beckett or Ionesco, or, nearer in time, Tristan Tzara's *Mouchoir de Nuages* (1924)?[22]

Interestingly, in Ovid the account of the prophet's sex-change is immediately followed by the stories of Narcissus and Pentheus, both of whose fates he foretold. The narcissist and the self-repressed voyeur. Ovid understood that it is Tiresias who stands behind them, he who has, in Eliot's words, "foresuffered all / Enacted on this same divan or bed".

The **Narcissus** myth embodies suffering of a distinctive and exquisite kind. Ovid relates, in rapt terms, the familiar story of the beautiful youth who falls in love with his own reflection. With psychological acuity, Milton adapted these

---

[22] Tzara dedicated this play to Nancy Cunard, who had come up with the title.

lines to conjure an image of the neonatal Eve, as a girl enamoured of herself. When first brought to life, she happens to catch sight of her own reflection:

Not distant far from thence a murmuring sound
Of waters issued from a cave, and spread
Into a liquid plain, then stood unmoved
Pure as the expanse of Heaven; I thither went
With unexperienced thought, and laid me down
On the green bank, to look into the clear
Smooth lake, that to me seemed another sky.
As I bent down to look, just opposite
A shape within the watery gleam appeared,
Bending to look on me: I started back,
It started back; but pleased I soon returned,
Pleased it returned as soon with answering looks
Of sympathy and love: there I had fixed
Mine eyes till now, and pined with vain desire,
Had not a voice thus warned me…
[*Paradise Lost*, IV, 453-66; cf. *Metamorphoses*, III, 407-36]

At which point the voice of God leads her away from such vanity of vanities and she meets Adam for the first time "under a platane". Her first impression of her new consort is that he is "less fair, / Less winning soft, less amiably mild" than the reflection she has just been admiring. She turns as if to go back to the pool, until recalled by Adam to her theological destiny – to become his helpmeet and mother of the human race. Duly put in her place, she now accepts "How beauty is excelled by manly grace / And wisdom, which alone is truly fair."

The Greek travel writer Pausanias (2nd C. AD), un-convinced by the standard version, recorded a novel variant of the Narcissus story, in which the youth falls in love with his twin sister rather than himself:

[7] On the summit of Helicon is a small river called the Lamus. In the territory of the Thespians is a place called Donacon (Reed-bed). Here is the spring of Narcissus. They say that Narcissus looked into this water, and not understanding that he saw his own reflection, unconsciously fell in love with himself, and died of love at the spring. But it is utter stupidity to imagine that a man old enough to fall in love was incapable of distinguishing a man from a man's reflection.

[8] There is another story about Narcissus, less popular indeed than the other, but not without some support. It is said that Narcissus had a twin sister; they were exactly alike in appearance, their hair was the same, they wore similar clothes, and went hunting together. The story goes on that Narcissus fell in love with his sister, and when the girl died, would go to the spring, knowing that it was his reflection that he saw, but in spite of this knowledge finding some relief for his love in imagining that he saw, not his own reflection, but the likeness of his sister. [Description of Greece, 9.31, tr. Jones/Ormerod, 1918]

For some, Narcissus may appear a model of self-sufficiency. More commonly, he exemplifies frustration, a life unfulfilled. Marina Warner eloquently describes the downside of his yearning:

Because the face, and most especially the eyes, cannot look at themselves except in reflection, reflections in the glass conflate self as subject and self as object into an insoluble enigma, as the myth of Narcissus so powerfully (and piteously) dramatizes. For while the self appears detached and bounded in the mirror, any move or gesture changes the image accordingly, through that indissoluble twinship that makes Ovid's Narcissus cry out in agony when he cannot reach his beloved alter. This extreme doubling turns the field of the visible into an extension of the beholder: a state akin to extreme delusion and mental disturbance.[23]

The Narcissus myth illustrates the frustration of using a mirror. While the self in a mirror may appear "detached and bounded", like a puppet it can only move when you move; like an automaton it can only imitate your movements. However, in one intriguing sense it's physically different from you: if you're right-handed, your mirror-self is left-handed, and vice-versa.

The third character linked in Ovid's narrative is, perhaps, best known as the central figure of Euripides' great tragedy *The Bacchae*. (Ovid's version differs slightly from his predecessor's.) The background is the cult of Dionysus as it spread from Asia to the Greek mainland. Dionysus, divine son of Zeus and the Theban Semele, induces the women of Thebes to celebrate his rituals on Mount Cithaeron. **Pentheus**, grandson of Cadmus and king of Thebes, refuses to allow Dionysus into the city, despite the remonstrances of the blind Tiresias, who warns him (in Ovid's version): "How lucky it would be for you, if you too were to be deprived of sight, so that you could not behold Bacchus' sacred rites!". Implacably hostile to the new religion, Pentheus attempts unsuccessfully to imprison the newcomer but is persuaded by the god in disguise to go up to the mountains to watch the Bacchic orgies. There he is killed and torn to pieces by the Theban women in their frenzy, led by his own mother, Agave, who only later realises the enormity of her actions. Pentheus is a complex figure, fearful of relaxing his self-control, yet drawn by fascinated curiosity to put on women's dress to spy on the bacchants. Are we to understand that his crude puritanism results

---

[23] *Phantasmagoria: Spirit Visions, Metaphors, and Media into the Twenty-first Century* (2006).

from a half-consciousness of his own Dionysiac nature?

Separately or together, these three mythological figures – Tiresias, Narcissus, Pentheus – lend themselves to many creative variations on gender and identity, two cultural preoccupations of the moment. For the novelist, composer, painter, sculptor, choreographer, the *maker* in whatever genre, it must be tempting to weave variations on these themes. I long to be of their number.

Blood for the Ghosts
A fiction

With a sigh, Sean Bowman opened the package and laid the contents on his desk. It had been a long day. A wad of closely typed pages, with a covering note.

This little volume contains the bulk of the fiction I wrote in the 1970s – not all of it, by any means, but everything I should wish to preserve. I haven't written any fiction for thirty years and I doubt I shall ever write any again. My motives for rescuing it from oblivion and dusting it down now are complex, various and, if I'm honest, not entirely creditable. But on re-reading this work, because it lies so far in the past, I had the sense that I was reading someone else, someone I once knew, which enabled me to approach it with a combination of objectivity and empathy I cannot feel towards anything I have written since.

What follows, I know, is young man's work, the product of someone who had read too much and lived too little. Nonetheless, my critical instincts, refined in the decades following, tell me that there is something of value here. What I felt between the ages of sixteen and twenty-two I shall never feel again, and whatever inspired these stories – call it 'divine afflatus' or just repressed emotion uncorked in an onrush of storytelling – has never visited me since. Beyond correcting one or two malapropisms, I have resisted the temptation to revise them in any way.

This was not promising. If there was one thing worse than the bushy-tailed aspirant, over-eager to ingratiate himself while assuring you he knows how valuable your time is, it was the merchant of indifference. "I am what I am; it is what it is; take it or leave it," they seemed to say. Sean made to add the bundle to his ever-growing slush pile when his eye was caught by the title of the first story: *'The Spittled Knife'*. Poetic. Well, pseudo-poetic. "Spittled" – was that even a word? He began reading.

Far out in the bay, where the waves grew wilder and it was deep enough to drown a man, you could still see a light – three or four candles, perhaps, silhouetting tiny shapes behind the criss-cross pattern of the window. The night was so cool and still that you could sit for hours out there, just watching. But soon you would tire of drifting, and want to row shorewards over the fluffy surf. If you did, and you hobbled across the stones to where the rutted track passed the cottages, you would surely trip and fall – old coiled ropes, great black nets spread along the foreshore, even little rowing-boats cast up against the sea-wall. There was no moon, only the bright light from the end cottage. But now the quiet was broken by the rise and fall of boozy voices. You might join them, if you needed a friend. For, in the pub, men were growing maudlin, three men in particular.

Show, don't tell. On principle, he tried to avoid giving advice to tyros, but if he did it would be: "ditch the noisy narrator; get down and dirty with your characters". Still, the fellow had a certain way with words. And there was something familiar about those words. He read quickly to the end.

"All lost," Jim from the headland was saying. "It's the wives and kiddies I feel sorry for. Still, we put out the nets just the same next day. Didn't catch much..."

"Never do. None of us do." Walter with the yellowed

moustache and grey tufts on his face. "None of us," he repeated slowly.

The third man was forever flickering in the light, so that Jim couldn't see his expression. Jim turned to him.

"Tomorrow, we're taking just the one boat. For safety, see."

"All right, I'll stay."

"We'll be needing you for the gutting, mind."

Closing-time. The publican was pushing and prodding the men of the sea. Like rusty barrels they had to be rolled out of the door. Some shouted goodbyes, others were still singing. Only Jim paused after the pub had emptied. The other man had slumped out of the candlelight, but his voice came out clear and resigned:

"I'll be there. With my knife."

The sea was just as calm at first light next morning. The man left behind was awake, and in his grunts and wheezing he remembered the words from the darkness. It was his knife he needed; he sought it, and found it. After fingering and solemn inspection, there was no doubt: it was the one. It needed cleaning, though. By the time he's made it sparkle, there was a little sun on the cliffs, but it still looked bitterly cold outside.

And it was. He hurried down to the shore, afraid to face the sea. He fancied he could see thick white blocks of ice on the skyline, but then the sun dazzled him again and the slabs seemed to melt. Awesome the sea looked, though, and try as he might, he couldn't spot the sluggish trawler.

Seven o'clock.

Three hours passed. The man still sat hunched in his sou'wester. Every now and then the spray would moisten his face, keep him alive. The water lapped at his feet; the swirl tugged at his knife, but he dozed on. The seabirds showed him no respect.

By midday he had slept enough. He thought again of the boat. Some catch! Then he noticed the blade running inshore, so he leaned out to fetch it. They had been gone for eight hours. But the blade was as good as ever – no harm done. Eight hours? No, they must be dead. He spat on the blade, and the sun disappeared behind a dark hulk of cloud. He had to wait before he could admire the spittled glint. And his friends were out there on a tranquil sea. Perhaps on submerged rocks; perhaps their bodies would stick on a shelf somewhere, so they would be spared the ignominy of down-down to the sea-floor. The man left behind was lucky. For some reason he was full of cheer as he picked his way back to the cottage.

Every morning he made a cosy little breakfast and thought his only thoughts: mementos, photographs, loving messages, people who used to be alive. Every day he polished what there was to polish and took pride in pleasing himself. He was cheerful with it. On Christmas morning he felt really snug in his snow-house, and instead of his dead people thoughts he took to telling himself consoling tales: about the little things he'd done, how sensible he'd been in opting out of the fatal journey, and how he'd lost interest in the weather.

The nights in the warm bed were blissful, too. Why had he ever craved companionship between the sheets? But when he fell asleep, the dreams would come and spoil everything. And the further he lived into January the worse it became. Wives, kids, Jim, Walter, fishermen with barely remembered names; all the dead ones came to wag their fingers at him. Why wasn't he on the sea-bed? Why was he so alive?

On one such night he began the plans for his own end. He got out everything that might be useful and laid it all on the table – each piece was scrutinised, but nothing was right. By the splut-tering candlelight he gazed at the instruments, set out like a row of teeth. And he hid from the thought. It had to be something more elaborate. It was not, in fact, until twilight the next morning that inspiration came, and only then could he let slip exhausted eyes. The smug sleep of Christmas-time had returned. He was to walk out onto the promontory and there make his gesture, his sacrifice.

And in the day that followed he did a lot of thinking about it. Yes, he would walk to the edge; then it would be up to them to make the first move. An easeful death, something to get excited about. Singing quietly to himself, rehearsing what lay ahead, he used up his life into late in the afternoon. Then it grew dark and he knew his time was coming near.

He still sang a little, but now he was croaking, and he grew angry with the creaks and squeaks of the woodwork for defying him. He was shaking, but still he looked forward, never back. About nine o'clock he made his decision. Maybe it was too wet a night for it – that hardly mattered – but they were waiting for him, after all. Tensed up till it hurt, he opened the door, ducking from the contents of the gutter as he did so.

On the sea, giant waves crashed one upon the other, beating against the rocks. Sometimes white streaks caught his eye, and he wondered whether they were really crests, or sea-gulls floundering in the last gasp of life. Further along the track, the sea-wrack stretched, intact, but bleached and drowned by the rain. And the man left behind could never escape the steady squelch he made at every step. He looked ahead and saw the welcoming promontory. Beyond it was a deserted lighthouse, and beyond that the open sea. It was as if he was seeing these things for the first time. His end was drawing him nearer.

As he tried to walk towards the edge, he could have surrendered to them straightaway, for the wind, full of sharp stones, was carrying him along, chiding him from behind. But when he did arrive, he was glad it was only a short jump. His clothes he would leave on, for fear of busybodies who might come snooping after him. Right. But there was no jump: no one came to fetch him; no one pushed him in. Self-slaughter is cowardly; evading it is cowardly. The man near the edge looked down again. Was there anyone left alive? He sat down. There were no ships now, just a wreck buffeting against the end of the promontory, which fell apart with every breaker and sank a little with every tide. He knew what vessel it was, and had known since his arrival on that neck of land. The flotsam was carried out on the waves and there were dead fish amongst the seaweed. He pulled himself back from the edge, straining to listen to the optimism of sea and wind. Now he was dragging himself back to the cottage, determined to live. There would be no sacrifice that day.

There was a commotion in there when he arrived. Three or four candles were burning at once, voices, alcohol, like a celebration. Wraiths, frighteningly life-like things, surrounded him as he walked in. One looked like Jim, another like Walter, and they all slapped him on the back with icy, translucent hands.

"So you made it then!" said one.

"Pity you weren't there. What a catch!" from another.

"You look half-dead, mate!" Walter's voice.

And the man they'd left behind waited for Jim to take them away. But no one made any move to go. Instead, they sat themselves down, swigging from half-empty bottles, eyes intent on the incomer. A row of pallid faces. One, two, three. Minutes passed. They were still there – no puffs of smoke, no sagging flesh.

"You still got your knife?" Jim asked. "If we go, there'll be no coming back. We can't start all over again..."

But before Jim could finish, the man who was alive leapt up, seized his knife from a top shelf, and madly stabbed at the ghosts. They dropped away one by one and were lost in a vortex, their cries spiralling downwards seconds later. There was no blood.

Sean put down the typescript, his hands shaking. Years, decades, before he got into the publishing game, he'd hoped to be a novelist himself. It was a part of him he'd suppressed – literally, when he bundled up his juvenilia and tossed it into a builder's skip outside a neighbour's house. Quickly he leafed through the other titles. 'The Child and the Spells', 'Dead to the Wide', 'Fragments of Another's Life'... All his. He reached for a bottle of scotch he kept in his bottom drawer for emergencies. It was warming against the back of his throat, but of little help. Had he so forgotten himself that he didn't recognise his own work? Had the carapace of cynicism so smothered him? He poured another glass. But where had they come from? The author signed himself "John Archer". John Archer… Sean Bowman…

He got up from the desk, swaying uncertainly, and walked across to the shredder in the corner of the office. As it powered up, he held the sheets over the machine.

No. He couldn't do it.

Newton and Supermac

In June 1980 I was a final-year student at Oxford University. Rather to my surprise, that year I carried off one of the University's more renowned essay prizes, the Stanhope Prize in history. My subject, equally surprising to me at this distance, was 'A Religious Source for Newton's Science?' I had been intrigued to read that this father-figure of scientific method spent as much time studying theology as he did science (or 'natural philosophy', as it was called in the seventeenth century) and wrote over a million words on biblical subjects. His interests ranged from miracles and prophecy to numerology and alchemy. He would calculate the dates of Old Testament books and analyse their texts to discover their authorship. My guarded conclusion was that while Newton's anti-trinitarian, deistic version of Christianity "did not conduct him in any easy fashion to his scientific discoveries, it warned him off those discoveries which were to be made by later generations."

The Stanhope Prize was created by the 5th Earl Stanhope in the 1850s, and previous winners had included John Buchan (1897) and Aldous Huxley (1916), so I could fancy myself in august company. The spoils of victory were twofold: prize money to be spent on books at Blackwell's – the books to be prettily embossed with the Earl's family crest – and an invitation to 'Encaenia'.

'Encaenia' is the annual ceremony at which the University confers honorary degrees and otherwise shows off its finery by processing through town in academical dress. The Stanhope winner, together with the under-graduate winners of the Arnold Prize, the Newdigate Prize for Poetry and one other (Latin Verse, if memory serves) were required to read short extracts, a paragraph or two, from their be-laurelled contributions as part of the ceremony. We four had a rehearsal the day before. The University Orator, a genial Welshman called John Griffith whose main job was to compose florid Latin eulogies of the honorands, took us through the procedure. We would stand in the balcony of the Sheldonian Theatre, two on each side, and read alternately, following a cue in the form of a nod from the Chancellor enthroned below. The Orator's only 'note' for me was to speak up. "It's nice stuff but we can't hear you!"

Encaenia was preceded by something called 'Lord Crewe's Benefaction' – a sort of indoor garden party at Wadham College, with peaches, strawberries and champagne. This was where we got our first sight of the worthies to be honoured. There was Donald Coggan, recently retired as Archbishop of Canterbury, who reminisced vaguely with us about his own student days. And then there was Mstislav Rostropovich, in town to receive a well-deserved D.Mus. One of my fellow laureates was an amateur cellist and desperate to meet his greatest hero. Emboldened, we four sidled over and attached ourselves to his group. I wish I could remember what 'Slava' said to us, but I recall a ready smile and mischief in his eyes signalling not a little pleasure at being the centre of attention.

Slightly tipsy, heady from our brush with celebrity, we then took up our positions in the Sheldonian. The University Chancellor was the then 86-year-old Harold Macmillan. Former prime minister, dubbed 'Supermac' by the press in his heyday, he seemed a very shrunken figure now. My first impression was that he was propped up by flunkies, rather like the Grand Lunar as described in H.G. Wells's *The First Men in the Moon*:

...a number of body-servants sustained and supported [his] little dwarfed body and its insect-jointed limbs shrivelled and white. The eyes stared down at me with a strange intensity, and the lower part of the swollen globe was wrinkled. Ineffectual-looking little hand-tentacles steadied this shape on the throne... I saw that shadowy attendants were busy spraying that great brain with a cooling spray, and patting and sustaining it.

But this is literature getting in the way of memory. Five years after this event Macmillan was still chipper enough to deliver his famous broadside against Margaret Thatcher's privatisation policy – usually known as the "selling off the family silver speech" (although the term he actually used, with a precision appropriate to his patrician background, was "selling off the *Georgian* silver"). What's certain is that his hearing was failing by 1980 and when the previous reader was still halfway through her reading, the old boy started nodding vigorously in my direction. She carried on reading. Supermac's nods grew more insistent. I feared that the shadowy attendants might have to spray that great brain with a cooling spray. Eventually she was finished, and I was on. I declaimed my opening paragraph. God knows what he (or Rostropovich) made of it. At least it wasn't in Latin:

Newton was quite emphatic on the point: "... Religion and philosophy are to be preserved distinct. We are not to introduce divine revelations into philosophy nor philosophical opinions into religion." And some modern commentators there are who have taken him at his word, asserting that there is no plausible link between Newton's theology and his science: "... the mind of man is a set of compartments; between some compartments there are broad open doors, between others tiny cracks and pinholes, between others no connection at all," writes Lawrence Stone. However, psychological studies of the creative mind – and Newton's achievement in science was no less formidable than the work of the greatest Renaissance artists – teach us to approach a scientist's *obiter dicta*, particularly remarks about his methodology and the sources of his 'inspiration', with the utmost caution. Great men are often the greatest self-deceivers. Thus it is that an entirely different line of argument has developed in Newton scholarship: in its most hesitant formulation it merely reinterprets Newton as saying, not that religion and natural philosophy are incommensurable, but that scientific opinions are not to be advanced as essential articles of religious belief; the more extreme version of this argument, which has a lineage reaching back to Ernst Mach, holds that Newton's entire scientific achievement was suggested and conditioned by his religious beliefs. It is this latter view which has become fashionable, and it is this view which we wish to examine. The scope for dispute is considerable. There can be no reconciliation between Cotes, first editor of the *Philosophiae Naturalis Principia Mathematica*, who believed Newton's "distinguished work" to be the "safest protection against the attacks of atheists", and a modern scholar, Alexandre Koyré, who foresees in the end of the "traditional opposition of becoming and being" an end to the qualitative distinction of heaven from earth and thus, necessarily, the inauguration of an age of unbelief. The question, then, which we wish to pose is this: in what measure, if at all, were Newton's scientific investigations directed, limited, or flatly contradicted by his religious cast of mind?

The Two Cultures

This story begins on 7 May 1959. The place is Cambridge, a university town with a venerable history of scientific research. A portly, middle-aged man approaches the lectern in the Senate House building to deliver a public lecture. Nothing unusual in that. The man was C.P. Snow, the title of his lecture 'The Two Cultures and the Scientific Revolution' – and it was to have an impact far beyond his immediate audience. In that respect, if no other, it turned out to be a highly *un*usual lecture. C.P. Snow perhaps needs some introduction, because as I discovered when talking to people about this topic, few under the age of forty have heard of him. He was the classic grammar-school boy – clever, bookish, starting without social advantages. He became a research scientist, a Civil Service Commissioner, a company director. After the Labour election victory in 1964 he received a life peerage and accepted Harold Wilson's invitation to become second-in-command at the newly established Ministry of Technology. But his wider reputation rested on his writings – he was a prolific novelist (books which seemed to give their readers the sense of decision-making among the mandarin classes in which he had moved) and controversialist. And he was famous – Flanders and Swann did a song about him. He was even the satirical butt of one of Peter Cook's 'E.L. Wisty' monologues of the 1960s.

So this was the guest lecturer who mounted the rostrum in 1959. The "two cultures" of his title were those of the "literary intellectuals" (as he called them) and of the natural scientists. These two groups, so he claimed, neither trusted nor understood one another, and the division between them threatened to undermine the urgent need to harness technology to alleviate the world's problems. His complaint was that the decision makers he had encountered in his public life had been almost exclusively educated at the ancient universities, where they had studied history, literature, classics, subjects which ill-equipped them for what his later boss would call the "white heat of the technological revolution". He detected an arrogance in these literary types. As he put it:

They still like to pretend that the traditional culture is the whole of 'culture', as though the natural order didn't exist. As though the exploration of the natural order was of no interest either in its own value or its consequences. As though the scientific edifice of the physical world was not, in its intellectual depth, complexity and articulation, the most beautiful and wonderful collective work of the mind of man.

They were the heirs of those generation of Victorians who turned away from the Industrial Revolution which was transforming their lives, and preferred to train their

young men for administration, for the Indian Empire, for the purpose of perpetuating the culture itself, but never in any circumstances to equip them to understand the revolution or take part in it.

Literary culture, he suggested, wishes the future did not exist. Scientists, by contrast, like the great Rutherford, under whom Snow had worked at the Cavendish Laboratory in the 1930s, scientists have the "future in their bones". He saw only one way out of this impasse – a rethinking of education, a reversal of the increasing specialisation which forced British schoolchildren at age 16 (if not before) to decide whether their chosen path was to be 'Arts' or 'Sciences'.

Sometimes ideas are not original, they are just timely. There was very little in Snow's lecture, as he later admitted, which had not been said by someone else. Perhaps the Establishment, poised on the brink of the convulsive social changes of the 1960s, were now sensitive to these ideas. Perhaps he achieved impact, as orators often do, by overstatement and bold antithesis. Crude as Snow's bipolar cultural scheme may be – and of course it left little room for the emerging 'social sciences' which broke through the middle in the 1960s – I still find it suggestive, and worth revisiting sixty years later.

Certain developments familiar to Snow have been irreversible: the specialisation of disciplines is a consequence of the explosion of knowledge, carrying with it a specialisation of vocabulary (although this latter has probably been exaggerated as one discipline insists on fencing itself off from another with its own jargon). There have been missed opportunities on both sides: until recently scientists seemed little interested in promoting themselves among non-specialists; equally, creative artists showed little interest in what science could do for them – except in the utilitarian sense, the sculptor's concern with metallurgy or geology, the composer's interest in electronics, the film-maker's attention to 'special effects'. The cultural divide is still perpetuated by the British education system, which has seen many changes since Snow's day, but not at A-level (it remains to be seen whether future reforms of A-levels will disrupt old allegiances, alliances and prejudices).

Of course, there have also been enormous cultural transformations in Britain since Snow's time. One of them is the changed media landscape. In Snow's day the cultural agenda was set from the 'top' down, by the 'great and the good' – that's how it was possible for a lecture delivered before a group of stuffed shirts at an old university to launch a catchphrase. Now we derive all our catchphrases from the TV, and our opinion-formers are footballers and supermodels. The opinion-formers whom C.P. Snow characterised as the "literary intelligentsia" were a coterie of authors and essayists who met at publishers' parties in Chelsea, reviewed each other's books, and discussed the latest talk on the Third Programme. Such chatter probably still goes on, in attenuated form, but few are listening: following the expansion of the universities in the 1960s (which Snow strongly supported) literary discussion has become largely academicised (and marginalised); and the only person in recent times who could propel a 'literary' novelist on to the news agenda was the Ayatollah Khomeini, when he issued his *fatwa* against Salman Rushdie. Nowadays the sphere of 'culture clash' is between the mass media and the continuing scientific enterprise. Most people get most of their ideas about science nowadays from television, a medium still in its infancy when Snow was lecturing. Measured in hours of output, there is considerably more coverage of science on terrestrial television than there is of the arts – some of it good, some irritatingly bad, all of it now governed by the precept that, however complex the subject, the viewer has a maximum attention span of about fifteen seconds.

When did this divide between sciences and arts begin? The idea would have meant nothing to the poet John Donne. Writing in the early seventeenth century before technical vocabulary had taken off, he found the language of science mysterious and sonorous, and available. He could think of love, and of the scientific methods for determining latitude and longitude, as compatible and mutually enriching:

How great love is, presence best trial makes
But absence tries how long this love will be;
To take a latitude
Sun, or stars, are fitliest viewed
At their brightest, but to conclude
Of longitudes, what other way have we,
But to mark when, and where, the dark eclipses be?

In the eighteenth century the study of the natural world was still referred to as 'natural philosophy', one element in the all-embracing enterprise of 'philosophy'. The Encyclopédie, that great monument of the Enlightenment, surveyed knowledge on the assumption that the study of human affairs and the study of the natural world formed a continuum. The fissure really dates from that explosion of energy in the arts at the end of the eighteenth century which we call Romanticism. Rejecting the ordered rationality of the Enlightenment, Romantics turned to the emotional directness of personal experience and to the boundlessness of individual imagination. These are the lofty definitions you'll find in literary histories. Much better to illustrate this. Here is the young Samuel Taylor Coleridge describing a walking tour of Wales in 1794:

From Llanvunnog we walked over the mountains to Bala – most sublimely terrible! It was scorchingly hot – I applied my mouth ever and anon to the side of the Rocks and sucked in draughts of Water cold as Ice, and clear as infant Diamonds in their embryo Dew! The rugged and stony Clefts are stupendous – and in winter must form Cataracts most astonishing... I slept by the side of one an hour & more. As we descended the Mountain the Sun was reflected in the River that winded thro' the valley with insufferable Brightness – it rivalled the Sky.

Now, born from this emotional directness was a new hostility to science as something unemotional. This is from Alexander Gilchrist's *Life of William Blake*:

Some persons of a scientific turn were once discoursing pompously, and, to him, distastefully, about the incredible distance of the planets, the length of time light takes to travel to the earth, etc., when he burst out: "It is false. I walked the other evening to the end of the earth, and touched the sky with my finger"; perhaps with a little covert sophistry, meaning that he thrust his stick out into space, and that, had he stood upon the remotest star, he could do no more; the blue sky itself being but the limit of our bodily perceptions of the infinite which encompasses us. Scientific individuals would generally make him come out with something outrageous and unreasonable. For he had an indestructible animosity towards what, to his devout, old-world imagination, seemed the keen polar atmosphere of modern science. In society, once, a cultivated stranger, as a mark of polite attention, was showing him the first number of the Mechanic's Magazine. "Ah, sir," remarked Blake, with bland emphasis, "these things we artists HATE!"

Similar opinions are attributed to Keats in memoirs (despite his medical education) and find famous expression in his poem 'Lamia':

Do not all charms fly
At the mere touch of cold philosophy?
There was an awful rainbow once in heaven:
We know her woof, her texture; she is given
In the dull catalogue of common things.
Philosophy will clip an Angel's wings,
Conquer all mysteries by rule and line,
Empty the haunted air, and gnomed mine –
Unweave a rainbow, as it erewhile made
The tender-person'd Lamia melt into a shade.

(These lines need a bit of glossing. Keats is obviously using the word "awful" in its original sense, inspiring "awe" or dread. The modern meaning is first recorded in 1834, some years after Keats's death. "Gnomed" presumably means "inhabited by gnomes", "diminutive spirits fabled to inhabit the interior of the earth and to be the guardians of its treasures" [OED] – not irritating garden ornaments with fishing rods.)

Despite their hostility to mechanism, the English Romantic poets were immensely *interested* in science – and this is to their credit. We see this ambivalence in a letter Coleridge wrote in 1801:

My opinion is thus: that deep thinking is attainable only by a man of deep feeling, and that all truth is a species of revelation. The more I understand of Sir Isaac Newton's works, the more boldly I dare utter to my own mind, and therefore to you, that I believe the soul of 500 Sir Isaac Newtons would go to the making up of a Shakespeare or a Milton. But if it please the Almighty to grant me health, hope, and a steady mind (always the 3 clauses of my hourly prayers), before my 30th year I will thoroughly understand the whole of Newton's works. At present I must content myself with endeavouring to make myself entire master of his easier work, that on Optics. I am exceedingly delighted with the beauty and neatness of his experiments, and with the accuracy of his immediate deductions from them; but the opinions founded on his deductions, and indeed his whole theory is, I am persuaded, so exceedingly superficial as without impropriety to be deemed false. Newton was a mere materialist. Mind, in his system, is always passive, – a lazy looker-on on an external world. If the mind be not passive, if it be indeed made in God's image, and that, too, in the sublimest sense, the image of the Creator, there is ground for suspicion that any system built on the passiveness of the mind must be false, as a system. (To Tom Poole, 23 March 1801)

Fictional representations of scientists in Romantic literature (Frankenstein, Faust) are often transgressive figures – system breakers as much as system builders – reflecting their authors' troubled fascination with the new science. These poets were preoccupied with the natural world, and insofar as science extended our perspective on that world, they hoped to recruit science to their own purpose. Coleridge tells us that he attended Sir Humphry Davy's lectures at the Royal Institution "in order to renew my stock of metaphors." Wordsworth, while accepting an emergent two-cultures division, looks forward to their fruitful cooperation:

The remotest discoveries of the chemist, the botanist, or mineralogist, will be as proper objects of the poet's art as any upon which it can be employed, if the time should ever come when these things shall be familiar to us, and the relations under which they are contemplated by the followers of these respective sciences shall be manifestly and palpably material to us as enjoying and suffering human beings. If the time should ever come when what is now called science, thus familiarised to men, shall be ready to put on, as it were, a form of flesh and blood, the poet will lend his divine spirit to aid the transfiguration, and will welcome the being thus produced, as a dear and genuine inmate of the household of man. (Preface to Second Edition of *Lyrical Ballads* ([1800]))

But Wordsworth was jumping the gun. This didn't happen, or not for a hundred years. Instead, the nineteenth century witnessed an increasing specialisation in the sciences and a widening of the divide. In painting, the Pre-Raphaelite Brotherhood turned away from the machine age altogether and back to an idealised medieval past. The debate in the 1880s between T.H. Huxley and Matthew Arnold, the one defending science as a part of culture, the other doubting that science could produce an "educated man", was further confirmation of a growing divide.[24]

In this historical survey I want to roll on now to a period around 1930. As we have seen, these were formative years for Snow. In 1930, at the age of twenty-five, he was elected a Fellow of his college, Christ's. Among his Cambridge contemporaries were Humphrey Jennings, later to be a documentary film-maker and author of a documentary history of the Industrial Revolution, *Pandaemonium* (from which I've drawn a number of my quotations), and a young Polish exile named Jacob Bronowski. Arts and sciences (at this time, in this place) were in dialogue: Jennings, the English Literature undergraduate, and Bronowski, then a mathematician, co-founded a journal called *Experiment*. It was a great age for popular scientific writing: Arthur Eddington, James Jeans, Julian Huxley were all active. But these young men's landscape was dominated by two imaginative writers whose every new book aroused intense discussion: H.G. Wells and Aldous Huxley. In these two figures, turgid as they can sometimes be in their prose, was a part fulfilment of Wordsworth's ambition to unite the sensibilities of poet and scientist. It is often assumed that Wells and Aldous Huxley were at loggerheads, that Huxley's *Brave New World* (1932), with its test-tube babies, its cult of sensation, its separation of sex from procreation, is a satire on the progressive utopianism expressed by Wells in, for example, *Men Like Gods* (1923), with its cheery vision of a future without overpopulation, prisons, police or party politics. In reality, as we have learnt from some recent scholarship, Huxley was very close to Wells's thinking at this time, the early Thirties. Both writers were dismayed by

---

[24] For more on Arnold see the essay on Aldous Huxley earlier in this volume.

what they perceived as the failings of parliamentary democracy and were convinced that civilisation must be reconfigured as an *aristocracy of intellect* if it was to stand any chance of survival. Both were seriously attracted to eugenics (a respectable cause at the time). These were momentous times in our national life: 1931 saw the formation of Britain's first National Government and the abandonment of the Gold Standard. Huxley was impressed by Oswald Mosley's call for a "strong executive" free from obstruction by Parliament. All were agreed on the need for systematic national planning. Reviewing Wells's *Experiment in Autobiography* in 1934, C.P. Snow made clear his admiration for this "great writer" and his sympathy with Wells's "urge for a planned world".

Why draw attention to a small group of Dead White Males in one place at one time? It is to try to position Snow in the intellectual constellation of his youth. In 1959 he imagines that the 'Two Cultures' divide will be healed by a new class of scientific administrators, a meritocracy unencumbered by traditional social attitudes – people, one supposes, not unlike himself. These ideas, I suggest, revert to the schemes for 'World Government' and authoritarian central planning he had read about and espoused in the 1930s

In fact there were much more attractive, and less dogmatic, commentators on the two-cultures issue than Snow. One such was his contemporary Jacob Bronowski. During the Second World War Bronowski pioneered the use of mathematical theory to increase the effectiveness of bombing raids. He was sent to Japan in 1945 to study the effects of the atomic bomb on Nagasaki. This experience clearly changed his life; he gave up military research to concentrate on the life sciences and the ethics of science. As a teenager I was enthralled by Bronowski's television series, *The Ascent of Man* (made just before his death) – I suppose if anyone could have turned me into a scientist, it would have been Bronowski. Unfortunately, he was not my teacher and I was repelled by the mind-numbingly dull science teaching we received at school. I don't know whether Bronowski ever wrote about Snow – I've not come across anything. But in the last programme of *The Ascent of Man* he talks about his friend, John von Neumann, mathematician and one of the founders of computer science, and I suspect that his gentle strictures on Neumann might apply to Snow as well:

Johnny von Neumann was in love with the aristocracy of the intellect. And that is a belief which can only destroy the civilisation that we know. If we are anything, we must be a democracy of the intellect. We must not perish by the distance between people and government, between people and power, by which Babylon and Egypt and Rome failed. And that distance can only be conflated, can only be closed, if knowledge sits in the homes and heads of people with no ambition to control others, and not up in the isolated seats of power.

"A *democracy* of the intellect" – this was Bronowski's ideal of cultural renewal, no doubt fostered by the many years he spent in America, at the Salk Institute for Biological Studies in California. He was well-attuned to the post-war spirit, probably better than Snow. He understood the potential of television for democratising intellect:

Television is an admirable medium for exposition in several ways: powerful and immediate to the eye, able to take the spectator bodily into the places and processes that are described, and conversational enough to make him conscious that what he witnesses are not events but the actions of people. [...] Unlike a lecture or a cinema show, television is not directed to crowds. It is addressed to two or three people in a room, as conversation face to face – a one-sided conversation for the most part, as the book is, but homely and Socratic nevertheless. To me, absorbed in the philosophic undercurrents of knowledge, this is the most attractive gift of television, by which it may yet become as persuasive an intellectual force as the book.

One scene from the series (made in 1973) lodges in my memory. This is the last four minutes or so of a programme called 'Knowledge or Certainty'. Bronowski highlights the irony that just at the moment Heisenberg was enunciating his 'Uncertainty Principle' in physics, Europe saw the rise of dictators who arrogated to themselves a "principle of monstrous certainty", then continues:

[voice over]
There are two parts to the human dilemma. One is the belief that the end justifies the means. That push-button philosophy, that deliberate deafness to suffering, has become the monster in the war machine. The other is the betrayal of the human spirit: the assertion of dogma that closes the mind, and turns a nation, a civilisation, into a regiment of ghosts – obedient ghosts, or tortured ghosts.

[at Auschwitz; to camera]
It is said that science will dehumanise people and turn them into numbers. That is false, tragically false. Look for yourself. This is the concentration camp and crematorium at Auschwitz. This is where people were turned into numbers. [...] And that was not done by gas. It was done by arrogance. It was done by dogma. It was done by ignorance. When people believe that they have absolute knowledge, with no test in reality, this is how they behave. This is what men do when they aspire to the knowledge of gods. Science is a very human form of knowledge. We are always at the brink of the known, we always feel forward for what is to be hoped. Every judgment in science stands on the edge of error, and is personal. Science is a tribute to what we can know

although we are fallible. In the end the words were said by Oliver Cromwell: "I beseech you, in the bowels of Christ, think it possible you may be mistaken." I owe it as a scientist [...], I owe it as a human being to the many members of my family who died at Auschwitz, to stand here by the pond as a survivor and a witness. We have to cure ourselves of the itch for absolute knowledge and power. We have to close the distance between the push-button order and the human act.

Bronowski arrived in England at the age of twelve, speaking, so he tells us, rather badly two words of English which he had picked up on the Channel ferry. Over the next few years he mastered his new language and read "with a perpetual sense of discovering a new and, I slowly realised, a great literature." He speculates that the difficulties he faced when encountering English literature were precisely those that "intelligent people today have in trying to make some order out of modern science." As he commuted between science and literature (his output included an important biography of William Blake in addition to scientific writings), he exemplified a kind of cultural bilingualism. He wrote in *The Common Sense of Science*:

Here in fact is one of the few psychological discoveries of our generation to which we can hold with a reasonable certainty: that the general configuration of intelligence factors which distinguish the bright from the dull is the same in one man as another, in the humanist as in the scientist. We are divided by schooling and experience; and we differ, though we differ less, in our aptitudes; but below these, we share a deeper basis of common ability.

In other words, why can we not be bi-lingual in the language of art and the language of science?

One creative artist who responded to Bronowski's syncretic vision was the composer Michael Tippett. Tippett was of the same generation as Snow and Bronowski. As a student at the Royal College of Music in the Twenties he read H.G. Wells's *Men Like Gods* and was much enamoured of its presentation of a future scientific utopia. One of his earliest efforts at composition was a piece for chorus and orchestra based on a didactic passage about Time in that book. Sixty years later his vast choral work *The Mask of Time*, premiered in Boston in 1984, is explicitly inspired by, and sometimes textually dependent on, *The Ascent of Man*. (Tippett was a real TV junkie in old age – photographs of him show an octogenarian couch potato curled up on the sofa watching the latest soaps.) Thus, for example, one movement of *The Mask of Time*, called 'Mirror of Whitening Light', is directly related to an earlier programme in Bronowski's series where he describes the advance from the primitive processes of the first coppersmiths, through the magical speculations of the alchemists to the discovery of the atom. Tippett and Bronowski were not, however, identical in their viewpoints. For Bronowski the scientific achievements of the twentieth century justify confidence in the future 'ascent of man', notwithstanding the catastrophes of two world wars. Tippett was more cautious, more sceptical. He believed that as an artist he had to defend values which were in danger of being ignored or obliterated by societies which had put their economic resources primarily at the disposal of technology.

So much for a generation born around 1900, who came to maturity in the inter-war years and were elevated to 'public figures' (like Snow) or 'gurus' (like Aldous Huxley, posthumously) in the 1960s. What of the present, now shaped by those born since 1945? There is one point of similarity with the early 1930s (and I don't mean declining respect for Parliament). We are once again in a golden age of popular scientific writing. On any station bookstall you'll find books by Stephen Jay Gould, Stephen Weinberg, Steven Rose, Stephen Hawking, Steve Jones (why are these men all called 'Stephen'?) Their business is to explain complicated ideas in an accessible form to non-specialist readers, especially those on the other side of the two cultures divide. When they succeed they are the true torch-bearers for Bronowski's ideal of a "democracy of the intellect". Though I'm sure they have an eye to their bank balances as well, they are to be welcomed as part of the 'public understanding of science' movement which has mushroomed in recent years. Richard Dawkins, formerly Professor of the 'Public Understanding of Science' at Oxford, sets out an agenda for the 'appreciation' of science by non-scientists, using an analogy with music (the best artform to choose, since often scientists with no other artistic interests will be music-lovers). It is indisputable, says Dawkins in his book *Unweaving the Rainbow*, that someone can enjoy the Mozart Clarinet Concerto without being able to play the clarinet:

Couldn't we learn to think of science in the same way? It is certainly important that some people, indeed some of our brightest and best, should learn to do science as a practical subject. But couldn't we also teach science as something to read and rejoice in, like learning how to listen to music rather than slaving over five-finger exercises in order to play it?

Consider the implications of that suggestion. At one level it might be a call for a 'holistic' world view. This has been advanced by another of the new popularisers, Edward O. Wilson, a Harvard biologist, in his book *Consilience: The Unity of Knowledge*. As he puts it:

The human condition is the most important frontier of the natural sciences. Conversely, the material world exposed by the natural sciences is the most important frontier of the social sciences and humanities [...] The two frontiers are the same.

According to Wilson, there should be no 'Two Cultures' divide, for sciences and arts have a common goal:

The central idea of the consilience world view (the word means 'jumping together') is that all tangible phenomena, from the birth of stars to the workings of social institutions, are based on material processes that are ultimately reducible, however long and tortuous the sequences, to the laws of physics.

My hackles rise when I hear that word 'reducible'. Reductivism is what troubled Blake and Keats about Newton, what troubled Tippett about science. And sure enough, when we turn to what Wilson says of the arts we find him espousing the new fad of biopoetics or bio-aesthetics, which holds that all innovation (including artistic) is a concrete biological process founded on nerve circuitry and neurotransmitter release. Up to a point this approach is helpful. In literary criticism it may help us to understand the ubiquity of archetypal mythic con-figurations – why do the same stories, the same figures recur in Babylonian Epic, medieval romance, James Joyce's *Ulysses*? It may help to understand the paradox of musical modernism. Why, a hundred years after Schoen-berg's push into atonality, has the public not 'caught up' with him? Why is it that the only use for atonal music that has been found in popular culture is in horror movie scores? A friend of mine proposed writing a book called *Reading Dissonance* – as he described it, "a subversive history of modern music which deals with the impossibility of discarding the basic human psycho-acoustic reactions to unpleasant sounds which modernism presumed could be simply suppressed." (Alas, it has yet to see the light of day.)

The fact that the only contemporary 'classical' composers who can fill a concert hall are those who have variously distanced themselves from modernist orthodoxies – Arvo Pärt, John Taverner, James MacMillan, Philip Glass – lends validity to such musical 'bioaesthetics'. However, Wilson's reductive bioaesthetics is not enough. It does not account for that residue, which to science is merely the 'not yet known' but which in art may be the defining characteristic of an artwork. For critical appreciation of the arts we need a much wider range of styles and methods of interpretation than Wilson's scheme permits. And even if we could stomach the reductivism of Wilson's approach, there is still the arrogance. Arrogance, I fear, is the other hubristic sin with which scientists stand charged. That damned impudence, to suppose that everything is knowable, had we but world enough and computing power!

I propose instead that the two cultures should meet in a spirit of humility. No one, not even Edward O. Wilson, knows why Mozart's piano concertos are immensely more satisfying and life-enhancing than Schoenberg's Piano Concerto. In a properly 'bi-lingual' culture, those with an arts background would have an insight into scientific method which would better equip them to understand the calculation of risk and 'safety', the need for hypothesis, experiment and innovation. They would stop delivering Luddite tirades against technology into their mobile phones while fingering the upholstery of their BMWs. Then, newly humbled, sciences and arts might discover the wisdom of Wordsworth's consilience:

We have no knowledge, that is, no general principles drawn from the contemplation of particular facts, but what has been built up by pleasure, and exists in us by pleasure alone [...] The knowledge both of the poet and the man of science is pleasure.

Knowledge should be pleasurable, by whatever cultural conduit it reaches us. Even as an outsider, I recognise how scientific research could be pleasurable. I see also how it might inspire awe. We remember that Keats believed his "awful rainbow" to have been unwoven by science. This is a misprision. Science, approached with a certain humility, could actually enhance our sense of awe, as Carl Sagan observed in his book *Pale Blue Dot*:

How is it that hardly any major religion has looked at science and concluded, "This is better than we thought! The Universe is much bigger than our prophets said, grander, more subtle, more elegant"? Instead they say, "No, no, no! My god is a little god, and I want him to stay that way." A religion. old or new, that stressed the magnificence of the Universe as revealed by modern science might be able to draw forth reserves of reverence and awe hardly tapped by the conventional faiths.

I want to commend to the attention of the arts community two sciences which might restore a taste for *wonder* to palates jaded by a decades-long diet of 'postmodernism' and 'deconstruction'. One is Sagan's own speciality – astronomy; the other, the science that probably touches the lives of every one of us – computing and information technology. First, astronomy. Growing up in the Seventies, I like many others was disillusioned by the anti-climax of the moon landings. "We went to the moon, and all we did was pee on it" (as someone said – I forget who). The reorientation of NASA's priorities after that – and the shrinking budget – has, I think, inaugurated a much more exciting phase in space exploration: unmanned probes visiting the outer planets, the Hubble telescope, the SETI project (scanning the skies for radio signals which might signal intelligent life). Take the images from the Voyager missions and the Galileo orbiter of the moons of Jupiter –

sights that no human eye had ever seen before. Io, a world covered in fresh layers of white, red, yellow and black patches, all different kinds of rock and sulphur compounds. Io is volcanically active, far more so than the earth. Europa, coated with a shell of ice which is thought to overlie a near-global ocean that in spots may be no more than 10 km from the surface. On its surface crisscrossing ridges may be the pathways for watery or slushy eruptions from below. The newest frontier in astronomy tells of planets we cannot yet see, but whose existence has been verified. These are planets orbiting other stars. Over four thousand have now been discovered. I recall a TV documentary that well conveyed the excitement of the British team who discovered a planet circling Tau Boo, 55 light years from Earth. The world they had discovered was "aweful" enough to wake any Romantic poet from his opium-induced reveries. Tau Boo's planet orbits 20 times closer to the star than Earth orbits the sun. Blasted by radiation, the atmospheric temperature is about 1,700 degrees C. The reflected starlight has a blue-green hue, caused possibly by sodium vapour above clouds of magnesium silicate, a chemical which forms solid rock on Earth but is vaporised by the temperatures on this alien world.

My second example is the computer revolution. We may not realise it but we are probably living through another Industrial Revolution, with implications as momentous as the first. I would like to think that even now some latterday Humphrey Jennings is compiling a new 'Pandaemonium', documenting the "coming of the computer as seen by contemporary observers". Such a documentary would reveal that the "literary intellectuals" greeted this second revolution with a good deal more enthusiasm than they did the first. Hey, computers are just tools, aren't they, we all use them. How can they inspire awe? We all recognise that our home computer is obsolescent practically before we've unpacked it from the box. Computers double in power roughly every 18 months, a statistic that has held remarkably steady for the last 30 years. You don't have to be a statistician to realise that eventually they will match the computing power of the human brain – and then surpass it. This was predicted in the 1950s by Bronowski's friend John von Neumann, who commented on the "ever-accelerating progress of technology and changes in the mode of human life, which gives the appearance of approaching some essential singularity in the history of the race beyond which human affairs, as we know them, could not continue." 'Singularity' is a term from mathematics describing (if I understand correctly) a point at which rules fail, quantities become infinite, the curve rips through the graph paper. Neumann's 'singularity' should be precisely the subject matter of intelligent fiction for some new-fledged Aldous Huxley. Soon the rate of change will become so rapid that we will be unable to make any confident predictions about the day after tomorrow. We shall feel, in Lady Macbeth's words, "the future in the instant". The present will be squeezed ever tighter as the future impacts against us like a speeding train. And what, then, of the past? The book culture on which Snow and Huxley, Bronowski and Tippett were nurtured, will end up in the museum. In its highest potential the internet is "democracy of the intellect" in action – millions of voices, millions of opinions. At its worst, well, I recall a meme that circulated online (where else?) a few years ago. It went something like this:

A time-traveller from the present voyages back to the nineteenth century (physicists tell us that, if this feat were possible at all, you could only go backwards, not forwards). There he encounters an open-minded Victorian scientist. The traveller tells him about the internet. The Victorian's jaw drops. "Why, sir," he says, "this is surely the greatest boon to civilisation yet devised. To what principal purpose, may I ask, do your men of learning apply this stupendous engine?" "Well, let's see," replies the traveller. "Mostly we use it for sharing funny pictures of cats and getting into pointless arguments with total strangers."

In short, triggered by the IT Revolution, the cultural transformations of the next fifty years will be so massive as to render the 'Two Cultures' debate, like so much of the intellectual baggage of the last fifty years, redundant. What relationship will then exist between science and the arts?

I offer a modest proposal. Earlier in this essay I looked back to a period around 1800, when industrialisation and the advance of technical mastery threatened to alienate men and women from their connectedness to the natural world. Their reaction found literary expression in Romanticism. I pointed to immediacy of utterance, an attitude of wonder, a pleasure in knowledge as characteristic of that movement. Shelley puts it beautifully in his poem 'The Daemon of the World', when he projects a possible future in which human-kind gives up its separation from other forms of life and thereby discovers the fullest powers of mind:

All things are void of terror: man has lost
His desolating privilege, and stands
An equal amidst equals: happiness
And science dawn though late upon the earth.

"Desolating privilege" – marvellous phrase – is the desire to set ourselves apart from all other phenomena of the material world, to claim special status and to exercise control through knowledge. Shelley spotted the fault line developing between arts and sciences in the nineteenth century and looked forward to its healing. Perhaps that is the obligation we should take upon ourselves, two centuries later: to reinstate such Romantic notions as intuition, imagination and inspiration, and thereby to salvage our humanity in the face of what allegedly lies ahead of us – von Neumann's 'singularity', a future world where exponential progress is driven by greater-than-human artificial intelligence, truly a world fit for Mary Shelley's Frankenstein.

[This is an expanded and slightly updated version of a talk I gave as part of National Science Week at the House of Commons in March 2000.]

About the Author

Philip Ward is a writer, translator and (occasional) composer. He worked for many years in the House of Commons Library. A member of the Society of Authors and the Biographers' Club, he lives in Cambridge, UK, where he is a Senior Member of Wolfson College.

www.brushondrum.blogspot.com

www.ingramcontent.com/pod-product-compliance
Lightning Source LLC
Chambersburg PA
CBHW032117040426
42449CB00005B/180